A Williamson *Kids Can!*® Book

W9-BNR-732

AWESOME OCEAN SCIENCE!

INVESTIGATING THE SECRETS OF THE UNDERWATER WORLD

Cindy A. Littlefield

Illustrations by
Sarah Rakitin

WILLIAMSON PUBLISHING • CHARLOTTE, VERMONT

Library of Congress Cataloging-in-Publication Data

Littlefield, Cindy A., 1956-
  Awesome ocean science! : investigating the secrets of the underwater world / Cindy A. Littlefield ; illustrations by Sarah Rakitin.
    p. cm.
  "A Williamson kids can! book."
  Summary: Explores the wonders of the ocean, its floor, and the plants and animals that dwell in it, teaches how to protect these resources, and provides hands-on activities for further investigation
  Includes bibliographical references and index.
  Contents: You and the ocean — Water world — Currents & waves — Shorelines & tide pools — Sea life —The ocean floor.
  ISBN 1-885593-71-6 (pbk.)
  1. Marine sciences—Juvenile literature. [I. Ocean. 2. Oceanography—Experiments. 3. Marine ecology. 4. Marine animals. 5. Marine plants. 6. Experiments.] I. Rakitin, Sarah, ill. II. Title.
GC21.5.L58 2003
551.46—dc2l

2003033077

Kids Can!® series editor: **Susan Williamson**

Interior design: **Nancy-jo Funaro**

Interior illustrations: **Sarah Rakitin**

Cover design and illustrations: **Michael Kline**

Printing: **Capital City Press**

WILLIAMSON PUBLISHING CO.
P.O. Box 185   Charlotte, VT 05445
(800) 234-8791

Manufactured in the United States of America

1 0 9 8 7 6 5 4 3 2

Kids Can!®, *Little Hands*®, *Kaleidoscope Kids*®, *Quick Starts for Kids!*®, and *Tales Alive!*® are registered trademarks of Williamson Publishing.

Good Times™ and *You Can Do It!*™ are trademarks of Williamson Publishing.

DeDicatiⓞn

To my mom, Barbara, who showed me the merit of discerning when it's

best to go with the flow and when it's right to swim against the tide.

ACKnⓞWleDGMents

I'd like to thank my favorite conservationist, Jill Helterline, for enlightening me

about coastal ecosystems and for spending countless hours reminding decision

makers that something as powerful as the ocean can also be fragile.

Thanks, too, to the Littlefield family of Block Island and the

devoted members of the Committee for the Great Salt Pond

for illustrating what a true treasure it is to live by the sea.

Photography/Illustration: page 38: Algarve, Portugal, Susan Williamson; page 52: HMS *Challenger*, National Oceanic & Atmospheric Administration (NOAA) Photo Library/Steve Nicklas, from *The Voyage of the Challenger — The Atlantic*, Vol. 1, by Sir C. Wyville Thomson, 1878, p. 65; page 56: *Trieste II*, NOAA Photo Library, OAR/National Undersea Research Program (NURP); page 64: *Alvin* underwater, Woods Hole Oceanographic Institution (WHOI), © Rod Catanach; *Alvin* launch, WHOI, © Craig Dickson; page 71: The Biological Classification System, Michael Kline, *The Kids' Natural History Book* by Judy Press, p. 5; page 101: carnation coral, NOAA Photo Library, Mohammed Al Momany, Aqaba, Jordan; pillar coral, NOAA Photo Library, Florida Keys National Marine Sanctuary, Commander William Harrigan, NOAA Corps (ret.); sea fan and brain coral, NOAA Photo Library, Florida Keys National Marine Sanctuary, Steven Cook; elkhorn coral, NOAA Photo Library, Florida Keys National Marine Sanctuary, Paige Gill; page 104: rescuing oiled birds, NOAA Photo Library, *Exxon Valdez* Oil Spill Trustee Council.

Also by Cindy Littlefield

contents

BEGIN YOUR OCEAN ADVENTURE!

The ocean is a real celebrity! It's delivered memorable performances on the big screen, playing leading roles in *Jaws* and *Castaway*. It's made a splash in literary circles as a key character in the tales of *Moby Dick* and *The Old Man in the Sea*. Plus it's the featured artist in an extraordinary exhibit of coastal landscapes — breathtaking seaside cliffs carved out of clay and stone, and glistening beaches molded in all hues of pink, beige, white, and gray sand — currently on display all around the world.

All that, and the ocean still has time to dazzle audiences with a repertoire of magic tricks, such as evaporating into thin air and reappearing as a rainstorm or rolling up its seas to create "pipeline" waves for surfers to blast through at 30 mph (48 kph). No wonder the sea is such a popular hangout for all kinds of fascinating creatures:

birds in tuxedos, "cows" with whiskers, fish that turn on lights, and scores (make that schools) more!

If those aren't reasons enough to delve into the deep, consider this: The ocean's health is in *your* hands. It's true! Many of the things you decide to do and the *decisions you'll help make* will determine its fate. In a way, you and your friends are the future ambassadors of the ocean — the ones who will cast votes on important issues, such as how many more gallons (L) of oil can be pumped from underwater wells, and how many tons (t) of fish commercial boats can haul out of the water each year. Want to check it out for yourself? Climb aboard, Ambassador of the Ocean. This deep-sea adventure is about to begin — and it's guaranteed to be amazing!

Take 1

Awesome Ocean

Lights!

Camera!

Action!

THE MAGIC OF THE WATER WORLD

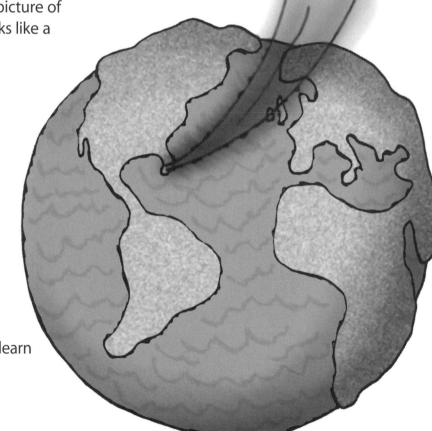

Sometimes, when something's really, really huge — an elephant, for example — you need to back up a bit to see the whole thing. In the case of the ocean, that would mean zooming out about 200 miles (322 km) into outer space! That's right. It wasn't until the 1980s, when the United States National Aeronautics and Space Administration (NASA) started sending space shuttles into orbit, that humans got a real picture of just how much ocean covers our planet. Earth essentially looks like a big blue ball of water speckled with a few patches of green and brown land, wrapped in swirls of white clouds.

It's all that blue that makes Earth such a unique place where life was able to develop and thrive. Other planets have water *vapor* (gas) and ice (solid), but not water in its liquid form — at least not much of it. Some scientists think that more than a million years ago Mars was covered with huge oceans filled with even more water per square mile (km) than here on planet Earth. But since the Martian atmosphere is way too thin to keep water from evaporating into space, the only liquid water left there today may be in underground pockets.

So how come our oceans stay filled? They're forever *recycling* themselves: Our atmosphere keeps the evaporated vapors from escaping. Stay tuned to discover why, while you learn about a whole world of ocean mysteries and science!

Oceans & Seas:
The Big Picture

A Wealth of Water

Q: What makes planet Earth the most people-friendly place in our solar system?

A: Its waves!

We humans just couldn't survive in a world without water (which makes up two-thirds of our bodies). Lucky for us, our planet is well supplied. More than 70 percent of its surface is covered with water — and practically all of it is in the oceans. With all that water sloshing around, it's no wonder Earth is a cool blue color when it's viewed from outer space.

Make Ocean Pie

A fun way to compare the ratio (proportions) of the earth's water to its land is to divvy up some delectable Ocean Pie. Before gobbling it up, take a good look at how much of it is red (land) and how much is blue (ocean).

Note: As with any recipe that requires using the oven or stove, be sure to ask an adult for permission before getting started.

- 9" (22.5 cm) piecrust (homemade or store bought), in pie pan
- 8 ounces (250 g) cream cheese, softened
- $\frac{1}{3}$ cup (75 ml) confectioners' sugar
- 2 tablespoons (30 ml) milk
- $1\frac{1}{2}$ teaspoons (7 ml) vanilla extract
- Whole strawberries, hulled (about 15 to 20)
- Blueberries (1 to $1\frac{1}{2}$ cups/250 to 375 ml)
- $\frac{1}{4}$ cup (50 ml) blueberry, strawberry, or apple jelly
- 1 tablespoon (15 ml) granulated sugar

Supplies: mixing bowl, electric mixer, measuring spoons, rubber spatula, empty pie pan, paper, pencil, ruler, small saucepan, wooden spoon, and pastry brush

WHAT YOU DO

1. Bake the piecrust according to the recipe or package directions. Let it cool completely.

2. Using the electric mixer, beat together the cream cheese, confectioners' sugar, milk, and 1 teaspoon (5 ml) of the vanilla extract until smooth. Spread the filling evenly in the cooled piecrust.

3. Turn the empty pie pan upside down on the paper and trace around it. Draw a line through the middle to divide the circle in half; then divide each half into five equal-sized wedges so you end up with 10 sections.

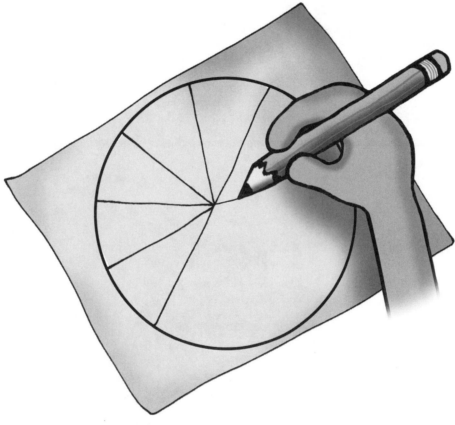

4. Choose three sections to be the earth's land area and pile on the strawberries. Transfer the fruit to the filling, arranging it any way you like into mountainous continents. That's it for land! Then, fill in all the uncovered areas with blueberry "oceans."

5. To make a glaze, heat the jelly and granulated sugar in the small saucepan, stirring occasionally. When the mixture bubbles, remove the pan from the stove, and stir in the remaining $\frac{1}{2}$ teaspoon (2 ml) of vanilla extract. Use a pastry brush to paint the glaze onto the blueberries so they'll glisten like the shining sea.

Now It's Blue — Now It's Not!

The next time you're at the beach, try your hand at a little seaside magic. First, take a minute to enjoy the beautiful view, noticing the ocean's deep blue color. Then, scoop up a pailful of water and presto! The "deep blue" is gone. How'd that happen? Well, the ocean water is colorless, just like tap water. That pretty blue hue we see is actually reflected light rays; but the volume (amount) of water in your pail is too small to reflect enough blue rays for it to appear blue.

Here's how it works.

Daylight, called *white light*, is really made up of *wavelengths* of colors. (Just hold one of your music CDs with the shiny side facing a lamp and you'll see the whole color *spectrum*: bands of red, orange, yellow, green, blue, indigo — deep blue — and violet. If that sounds like the rainbow, it is!) When white light shines on the ocean, all of those colors *except blue* are absorbed (taken in) by the water particles, so they seem to disappear! The blue rays bounce back, sort of like our images do from a mirror. The same thing happens whenever we see something blue, including the sky. So, on sunny days when the ocean reflects the sky above, it looks doubly blue!

Seawater can change colors, with a little help from Mother Nature. For example, the Yellow Sea, sandwiched between China and Korea, gets its tint from the muddy inflow of the Huang River (*huang* is the Chinese word for yellow). The Red Sea, bordering northeast Africa, is colored by crimson-colored algae. And the Black Sea, north of Turkey, owes its dark gray tint to hydrogen sulfide, a gas that smells like rotten eggs! (Ugh!) Can you guess how the White Sea got its name? Here's a hint: Located northwest of Russia, its surface temperatures drop as low as 27°F (-2.8°C), making it the coldest sea of all.

ONE, FOUR, OR FIVE: HOW MANY OCEANS ARE THERE, ANYWAY?

Seems like a simple enough question, but there's actually some debate over the answer. Some scientists say four; others claim five. The *Pacific*, which covers about one-third of the earth, is the biggest (you could fit all of the continents in it!). Next comes the *Atlantic* at just about half that size, followed by the *Indian*, which is relatively close in area to the Atlantic. That leaves the two polar oceans: the *Arctic* at the top of the globe and the controversial *Antarctic* at the bottom, which some geographers argue is not an ocean at all, but simply the southern portions of the Pacific, Atlantic, and Indian oceans. (Check it out on the map below — would you count it as an ocean?)

Then there are the *seas*, which are smaller bodies of salt water. Some are almost completely enclosed by land, such as the Mediterranean and Red seas. Others are parts of oceans generally associated with bordering countries, such as the East China Sea. If you counted seas as oceans, you'd bump the total up to a few dozen!

Or, you could go the other way. You could say there's one ocean and technically you'd be right. That's because all the oceans and seas are connected — the same water flows in and out of all of them.

Ignoring the names people have given to areas of salt water on the earth, how many oceans do *you* count?

Catch the Drift

To get an idea of just where and how the ocean and land fit into the layers of our planetary landscape, imagine a giant soft-boiled egg with a cracked shell. The yolk represents the earth's scorching center of melted metal (the core*). The egg white is like the layer of liquid rock (the* mantle*) that's wrapped around the core. And the eggshell is the hardened rock surface (the* crust*), broken into several sections called* plates. *On earth, some of those plates are covered with water, others with land — and they're all floating around on top of the mantle.*

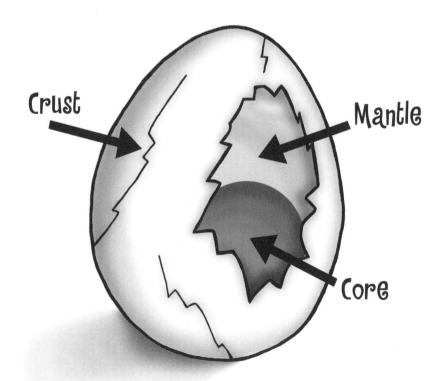

Crust

Mantle

Core

Ocean Lingo

salt water: Water that contains dissolved salts (much like the grains of common table salt on your kitchen table!). *Salinity* is the measure of the amount of salt in the water. The more *saline* water is, the saltier it is.

fresh water: Water that is not salty (doesn't have a lot of salts in it — less than one part salt per every thousand parts water, to be exact! In other words, nearly zero.).

ocean: The huge body of salt water that covers more than seven-tenths ($^7/_{10}$) of our planet's surface. All the world's oceans make up one super-gigantic ocean.

oceanographer: A scientist who studies the ocean and the plants and animals that live in it. (Sounds like fun, doesn't it? Perfect for an Ambassador of the Ocean, like you!)

sea: A word that's sometimes used to mean "ocean" and at other times names a particular *part* of an ocean that's bordered by land. (So the Arabian Sea is really part of the Indian Ocean, and the Caribbean Sea is part of the Atlantic Ocean.)

gulf: A part of the ocean that is partially enclosed by land, such as the Gulf of Mexico (formed by the southern border of the U.S. and the eastern border of Mexico).

sound: Yes a noise, but it's also a narrow passage of water between two bigger bodies of water or between a mainland and an island.

estuary: The wide part of a river's lower end (mouth) that empties out into the ocean. There, fresh water from the river mixes with the ocean's salt water, creating a special habitat for all sorts of wonderful creatures!

 tides: The rise and fall of the ocean waters caused by the gravitational pull of the moon and the sun on the earth. *High tides* come in twice a day, about every 12 hours. *Low tides* occur about 6 hours after the high tides.

Seems Like Magic:
The Water Cycle

So, how did the world get so wet in the first place? No one's completely sure, but here's what *geologists* (scientists who study everything about the earth) think: Billions of years ago, dust and gas particles in our galaxy, the Milky Way, clumped together and formed our sun and the planets around it. Then, as the earth grew, *meteorites* (pieces of rock that fall from outer space) slammed into it with so much force they melted its rocky parts. This continued for at least 500 million years!

Eventually, as fewer meteorites hit the earth, the planet's surface cooled and got crusty, but its center stayed really hot — hot enough to form volcanoes.

When the vapors blasting from those volcanoes cooled and *condensed* (turned from gas to liquid), things started getting kind of cloudy. Can you guess what happened next? Here's a hint: It's wet, it fell from the sky (for thousands of years without stopping!), and it eventually filled up the world's biggest and oldest in-ground swimming pools — the oceans!

Awesome Ocean Science!

Abracadabra: It's Raining in a Jar!

Guess what? The very same rain that fell billions of years ago on Tyrannosaurus rex *may have fallen on YOU yesterday! (Just think: dinosaur rain, or Abraham Lincoln rain, or rain that touched the pyramids of Ancient Egypt, or Babe Ruth rain!) That's right! The earth is the ultimate recycling machine. And that same rain rises, too, in the* form of water vapor as it evaporates from warmer temperatures. Then, it condenses in the air, forming clouds, and falls to the earth as rain again! This cycle goes on all over earth day in and day out. Want to see for yourself? Turn the page.

A Day in the Life of a Raindrop
(in three acts)

The Magic of Our Water World

WHAT YOU NEED

- Large wide-mouthed jar
- Hot water
- Ruler
- Plastic sandwich bag
- Rubber band
- Ice cubes or crushed ice

WHAT YOU DO

1. Fill the jar with about 2" (5 cm) of hot tap water for a mini tropical sea. Quickly insert the bottom of the sandwich bag into the top part of the jar and pull the top of the plastic over the rim, using a rubber band to hold it in place. Fill the bag with ice. Before long, the air in the jar will turn cloudy as the hot water evaporates, rises, and then condenses near the cold ice. But the best is yet to come!

2. Wait 15 or 20 minutes until the bottom of the plastic bag is covered with fat drops of water ready to rain down in the jar. If you just can't wait for them to fall on their own, go ahead and give the bag a little jiggle to get the shower started.

What's Happening?

The bag of ice keeps the water vapor from leaving the jar, just as the earth's atmosphere keeps the evaporating seawater from disappearing into space. That's why the same water flowing down the Mississippi River today may very well have washed ashore on Australia or snowed down in the Arctic one or more times in the past!

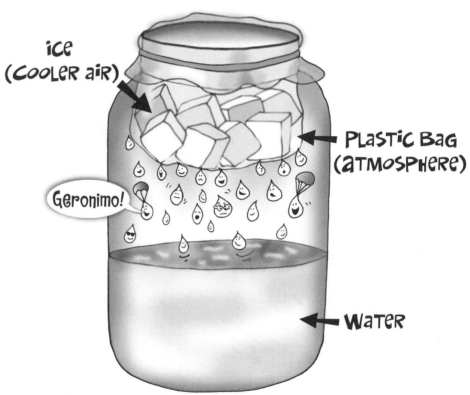

ICE (COOLER AIR)

PLASTIC BAG (ATMOSPHERE)

Geronimo!

WATER

OK, Ambassador of the Ocean: Can you explain the water cycle in your own words?

The Salty Sea

Rivers pour plenty of water into the ocean, too, but water isn't the only thing rivers carry. As they flow over rocks and soil, they pick up traces of *salt*. We all know what salt tastes like, but what is it exactly? It's a clear, brittle *mineral* (a natural substance that is neither a plant nor an animal) that usually forms perfect cubes — just look at a grain of salt under a magnifying glass to see! Once that salt gets into the ocean, it's there to stay. That's because water leaves the ocean only by *evaporating* into the air or by *freezing* into polar ice. Either way, it leaves its salt behind. Over time, the ocean's *salinity* (amount of salt) has become much higher than the salt content of the rivers.

Ride a River into the Ocean

At places where rivers empty into the ocean (estuaries), the fresh river water first forms a distinct layer on top of the more salty seawater. Then, with the help of the waves and tides, the two layers slowly mix together. This makes the water salty, but still less salty than the water in the open ocean — the perfect concentration for certain types of plants such as salt grass, eelgrass, sedge, and saltwort to grow. These plants provide food for different species of geese and ducks. Then, at the end of the growing season, other animals, such as worms, snails and clams, feed on the decaying plants.

WHAT YOU NEED

- Measuring cup with a spout
- Water (if your tap water is treated with a softener, use bottled water)
- Teaspoon
- Salt
- 20-ounce (600 ml) plastic soda bottle
- Old dish towel or rag
- Small plastic water bottle with a squirt nozzle
- Food coloring

WHAT YOU DO

1. In the measuring cup, combine 1/2 cup (125 ml) of water and 2 teaspoons (10 ml) of salt. Stir well to dissolve as much salt as possible.

2. Carefully pour the salt water into the soda bottle. Set the bottle on its side on top of the rag. This bottle is the salty ocean.

3. Fill the squirt bottle partway with fresh tap water and add enough food coloring to turn the water a dark shade when mixed in. This is the fresh river water.

4. Insert the squirt-bottle nozzle just inside the neck of the larger bottle. Gently squeeze the squirt bottle to start a slow, steady flow of colored water (the river) into the saltwater bottle (the ocean). What do you observe?

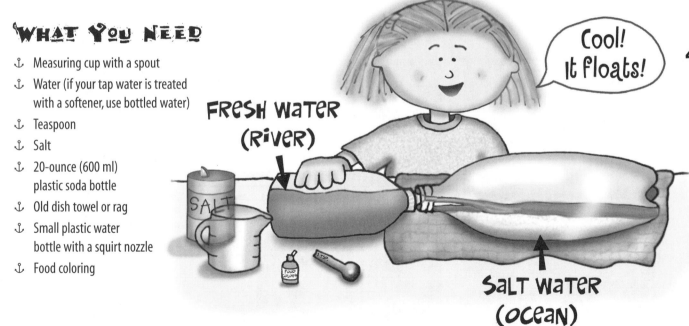

FRESH WATER (RIVER)

Cool! It floats!

SALT WATER (OCEAN)

Dive to the Bottom

Now that you've observed how fresh water floats on top of salt water, can you predict what salt water will do when you drop it into fresh water?

Try This! Fill a drinking glass halfway with fresh water. In a separate container, mix $1/4$ cup (50 ml) of water, 1 tablespoon (15 ml) of salt, and three or four drops of food coloring. Use an eyedropper to add the colored salt water, a drop at a time, to the fresh water. (If you don't have an eyedropper, you can dip one end of a drinking straw into the salt water and cap the other end with your thumb so the water is held in the straw; then use your thumb as a regulator.)

What's Happening?

The salty, colored drops fall straight to the bottom because they are much *denser* than the fresh water. *Density* is a measure of how closely the particles that make up a substance are packed together. In ocean water, dissolved salt particles fill in gaps between the water particles. So, salt water is denser than fresh because there are a greater number of particles packed into it.

Floating Made Easy

Have you ever noticed that it's a little easier to float or swim in the ocean than in a lake or pond? Because salt water is denser than fresh water, it increases your *buoyancy* (ability to stay afloat) by supporting your body weight a bit more than fresh water does. The water in the Dead Sea, between Israel and Jordan, is about seven times saltier than typical ocean water! That makes it nearly impossible for a person to sink there — and way too salty for fish to live in. (Get it? Dead Sea.)

Try This! Fill a tall drinking glass halfway with tap water and drop a chunk of raw carrot into it. Because the carrot is denser than the fresh water, it will sink straight to the bottom. Sprinkle in salt, ½ teaspoonful (2 ml) at a time (keep track of how many times you add salt), until the carrot begins to rise and stays *suspended* in the solution just above the bottom of the glass. Keep sprinkling in salt and watch the carrot — the more you add, the higher it will float until it reaches the top. How much salt did it take to make the water's density greater than the carrot's?

THE ICED SEA

Now you know ocean water gets saltier, but what makes it *less* salty? Well, there's rainwater (remember the water cycle, and there's another form of water: ice! Some of the ocean is really an "iced sea," and that ice has been melting for thousands of years.

During the last ice age (around 18,000 years ago), thick sheets of ice extended down from the North Pole, covering places as far south as today's New York and London! In the Southern Hemisphere, the tip of South America, as well as parts of Australia and Africa were under ice, too. Today, the largest ice sheets are found in Greenland and Antarctica. Significant glacial melt affects the salty ocean in two interesting ways: by raising the sea level and by diluting its saltiness. See for yourself.

Glacial Meltdown

What's the difference between the North and South poles? The North Pole is located on a huge sheet of sea ice in the Arctic Ocean — and there's no land under that ice! The South Pole is on Antarctica, a land continent. Surrounded by the Antarctic Ocean (page 10), this continent is almost completely covered by a glacier, a huge mass of ice formed by compacted snow. Here's the thing: If the ice on Antarctica melted, the ocean would rise. But if the sheet of Arctic ice melted, the water level would stay the same. What's up with that?

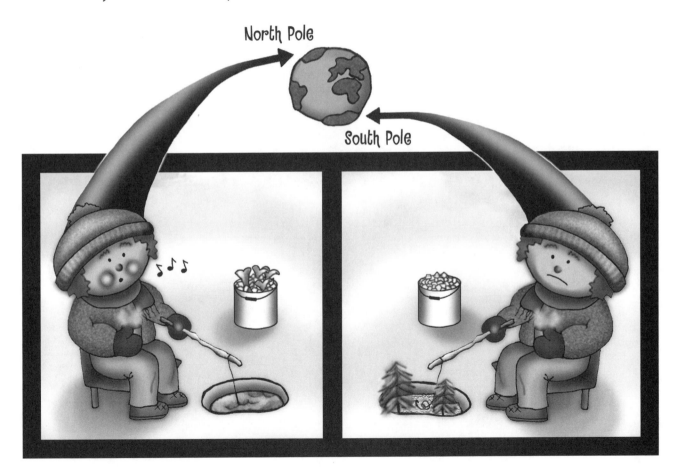

North Pole

South Pole

(page 10)

WHAT YOU NEED

- Permanent marker
- 2 unopened tuna cans
- 2 identical medium-sized bowls
- Crushed ice
- Pitcher of water

WHAT YOU DO

1. Make a mark in the same spot on both tuna can labels. Then, set the bowls side by side on a level surface and place a can in each one.

2. In the first bowl, pile as much crushed ice as possible on top of the can without letting any spill off. In the second bowl, sprinkle ice in the bowl around the can so that it comes about halfway up to the marked line. Carefully pour water into the bowls, stopping when you reach the mark on each label.

3. Give the ice time to melt completely; then recheck the water levels. Can you figure out why one rose and the other didn't? Hint: Keep in mind that the floating ice was already taking up space in the water before it started to melt.

What's Happening?

When the ice on top of the can melts, it trickles down into the water. This adds volume to the water in the bowl, making the level rise, just as the polar cap on Antarctica would raise the sea level if it were to melt. In the second bowl, the total volume of water remains the same when the ice melts. That's because nothing has been added; it just changed from solid ice to liquid water as it would do in the Arctic.

Glacial ice, on land (Antarctic)

Sea ice (Arctic)

Let the Great Melt-Off Begin!

Glacial ice melt raises sea level

Sea ice melt does not raise sea level

Ocean Gazette

March 17, 2000:
An Iceberg is Born

A piece of ice nearly the size of Texas broke off (or, as scientists say, was "calved") from Antarctica's Ross Ice Shelf today and set sail across the South Pacific. Iceberg B-15 (its official name) contains enough fresh water to supply the United States for five years! If only there were a way to get it there — or to another country in need — before it breaks into smaller icebergs and melts away into the salty ocean.

ICEBERG MAGIC: WHEN "SEEING" ISN'T BELIEVING!

Year after year, thousands of icebergs are calved from the polar ice caps. The ones that snap off the glacial land ice of Alaska, Greenland, and Antarctica tower into the sky like magical castles. Others that break away from the ice shelves around Antarctica (like B-15) are flat, like giant tabletops that stretch 50 miles (80 km) or more. But that's not the half of it! As the saying goes, it's "just the tip of the iceberg." See for yourself!

Try This! The next time you're planning a get-together with friends, serve iceberg punch. Beforehand, freeze a quart (L) carton of fruit juice. Once it's frozen solid, fill a punch bowl halfway with ginger ale or another light-colored soda. Briefly run warm water on the outside of the juice carton to loosen it; then peel it away and set the juice "berg" afloat in your soda sea. Notice that much of the juice iceberg is below sea — make that soda! — level. Up to about five-sixths of a real iceberg is underwater, too. No wonder ship captains are quick to steer clear whenever they see the "tip" of one.

Pancake Ice

One thing you can find plenty of in the Antarctic Ocean is pancakes. That's right, pancakes! Every winter (from April through November) when the temperatures average -22°F (-30° C), new ice forms in the waters around Antarctica. It starts as a thin sheet that resembles a grease slick (or maple syrup, if you prefer). Then, in spots, it thickens into frozen pancake-like disks that start to curl up around the edges. Small pancakes clump together forming bigger ones and so on, eventually creating a huge shelf called *pack ice*.

Ocean Gazette

April 15, 1912:
Titanic Cruise Ship Hits Iceberg and Sinks

After steaming into an iceberg in the North Atlantic, one of the world's largest and most luxurious cruise ocean liners, the Titanic, sunk at 2:20 A.M. today. Of the 2,208 passengers aboard, it's believed 1,503 have perished in the icy waters. The ship's lookout, Frederick Fleet, spotted the iceberg towering 100' (30 m) above sea level just 30 seconds prior to the crash. Six waterproof compartments in the starboard (right) side were punctured and, in less than three hours, the Titanic took on enough water to start her descent to the ocean floor. Engineers speculate that if the ship had hit the iceberg head on, it might have suffered minimal structural damage and stayed afloat.

MYSTERIOUS MOVES: WAVES & CURRENTS

Name a word that rhymes with *ocean* and describes it to a T. Here's a hint: It might be slow and easygoing, or fast and wild, but it never, ever stops. Give up? It's *motion*. Even on a calm day, when the surface of the water looks as smooth as glass, don't be deceived: The ocean is on the go. It's traveling around in circles, cruising along straightaways, rising up and down — all at the same time! In a way, the ocean is a world-sized water park with Mother Nature using the wind, the sun, the rotation of the earth — even underwater volcanoes and earthquakes — as the controls.

All that motion is more than a lot of commotion. It circulates heat around the planet and delivers food to all kinds of marine life — not to mention whipping up some awesome breakers for boogie boarding. So get ready to go on a wild ride of whirling currents, waves, and frothy surf.

Riding the Waves

When you see a wave out at sea, it may seem like the water is being carried along to another part of the ocean, but it's really not. *The water just moves up and down in place as the wave, which is actually energy, passes through.* In other words, the surface of the water changes shape, but pretty much stays in place! Think of a water bed. Push down on one spot and the area around it swells up. Remove your hand and the swell drops as the place you were pressing rises right back up. At the same time, you've started a wave, a rippling motion that travels all the way across the bed. That's just what happens when gusts of wind blow down on the ocean: The water falls and rises, as *waves of energy* form ridges and valleys that roll along its surface.

Q: How far does the water in a wave that begins 1 mile (1.6 km) out from shore travel to tickle your toes at the water's edge?

A: If you said 1 mile (1.6 km), which is a logical answer, then ... gotcha! The water in the wave doesn't travel at all! It is still a mile (km) away. It is *energy* that moves and causes the water to lap at your toes!

Try This! Want to make waves without even getting wet? Tie one end of a jump rope to a doorknob or the back of a chair and grasp the other end in your hand. Then move just far enough away to keep the rope from drooping. Start flicking your wrist up and down to send ripples down the line. Notice how neither you nor the rope has moved forward? The only thing that's moving is the energy that's passing from wave to wave.

So, what happens if there's something floating in the water — like you! — when, out of the blue, some big waves are headed your way? You're in for a ride, right? Right — a ride up and down, that is! *Waves make the water they're passing through rise and fall.* If you happen to be floating in deep wavy water, you'll feel as if you're on a liquid trampoline bouncing up and down in slow motion. When the water calms down again — surprise! — you'll pretty much be in the same spot where you started.

Try This! Draw a little face on a cork. Float the cork in the kitchen sink while you tap the water surface with a spatula to create waves. Other than bobbing up and down, does the cork move?

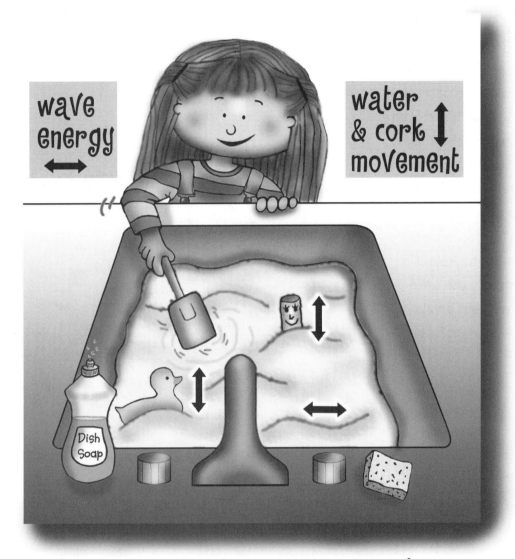

wave energy ←→

water & cork movement ↕

Dish Soap

Waves make the water they're passing through rise and fall.

Breakers in a Bottle

In deep water, wave energy can travel for thousands of miles (km) once it gets going. It isn't until it reaches a shallow place (like a beach) that it starts to slow down. There, the bottom of the wave starts to lose speed and drag along the ground while the top charges full speed ahead. Eventually, the wave curls over itself and breaks on the beach — perfect for body surfing!

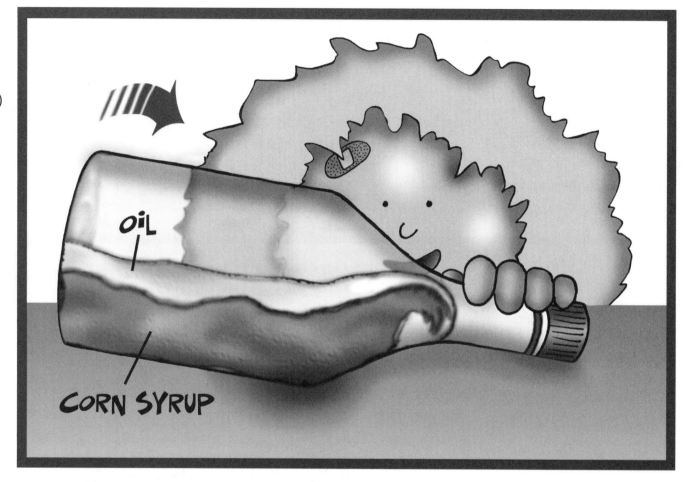

OIL

CORN SYRUP

Try This! Fill a tall, thin-necked bottle (like a ketchup bottle) a quarter of the way with corn syrup. (Water will do in a pinch, but corn syrup works much better.) Mix in a few drops of blue food coloring with the handle of a wooden spoon. Slowly pour in enough vegetable oil so the level reaches the middle of the bottle. Then, tightly cap the bottle and hold it on its side. Now slowly tilt the bottle so that the capped end points slightly down and watch carefully as the corn syrup flowing into the tapered neck begins to crest. Can you figure out how the bottle resembles a beach where real waves break on shore?

What's Happening?

Each time a wave in your mini ocean reaches the narrow bottle neck, it behaves just as a real wave does when it passes through shallow water along the shoreline. The lower portion of the wave slows down as it rubs against the sandy or rocky ground (or bottle in this case). The top of the wave rolls right along and topples over the lagging bottom, creating a breaker.

Fetching Waves

Want to stir up a batch of waves? Start with a good measure of wind and blow it across the ocean surface until you see peaks about 12' (3.5 m) tall. That's about as high as an average windblown wave gets.

When wind blows across a particularly large stretch of open, uninterrupted water (called a *fetch*), it can build some pretty awesome waves. That's why the Hawaiian coastline, which faces a huge fetch, is such an awesome surfing spot. Incoming waves rise to about 15' (4.5 m) and form long, hollow tubes called *pipelines* that adventurous surfers try to maneuver through. As the wave collapses, the compressed air can send a surfer shooting out of the pipe at about 30 mph (48 kph)!

TOWERING TSUNAMI

The biggest waves of all are started by underwater volcanoes or earthquakes — there's no wind involved at all! They're called *tsunamis* (tsoo-NA-mee), the Japanese word for "harbor" and "waves." (Sometimes they're referred to as *tidal waves*, although the tides have very little to do with their formation.) Once a tsunami begins, it can ripple out at a fast and furious 500 mph (800 kph) and build to more than 100' (30 m) high before crashing down on shore.

In the past 150 years, approximately 40 tsunamis have hit Hawaii. In 1952, an undersea earthquake near the Kamchatka Peninsula of Russia set a tsunami in motion that swept ashore on the Midway Islands (northwest of Hawaii), flooding streets and buildings. It rolled on across the Pacific, eventually reaching the Hawaiian Islands, where it destroyed boats and piers, lifted a bridge off its foundation, and threw a cement barge into a freighter! Today, organizations such as the Pacific Tsunami Warning Center (PTWC) in Ewa Beach, Hawaii, and the Alaska Tsunami Warning Center (ATWC) in Palmer, Alaska, continually monitor underwater activity and sea levels to detect major earthquakes and figure out if they've started a tsunami. With forewarning, coastal communities can prepare and minimize the effects of these sweeping walls of water.

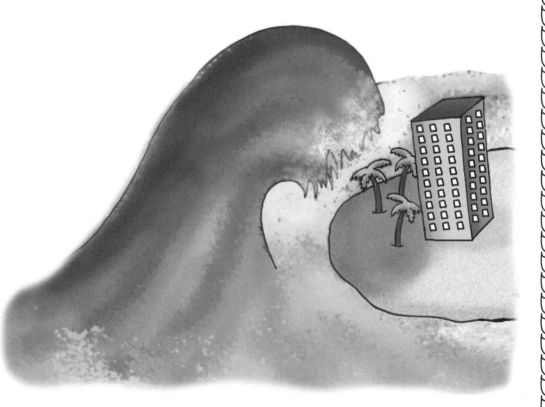

Cruising with the Invisible Currents

So, if waves just move water up and down, what moves water and everything in it (a message in a bottle, for instance) *across* the ocean?

Well, just as rivers flow on land, similar huge streams of water called *currents* travel through the ocean. Like expressways, they loop around in some places, stretch straight ahead in others, and even cross under and over one another. Currents that flow near the surface act like a giant combination furnace/air conditioner. Driven by the wind, these uppermost currents form huge circles that shuttle sun-warmed water from the tropics to both poles and cooler water from the poles back toward the equator.

Deep currents, on the other hand, start up when extra-cold, saltier water — particularly water near freezing ice — sinks to the ocean floor and pushes warmer, less salty water out of the way. Compared with surface currents, the deep currents are like very slow traffic lanes — it takes about 275 years for deep-current cold water from the poles to cross the Atlantic and 500 years for deep currents to cross the Pacific!

Fast or slow, though, *currents move water and objects across the ocean.*

Watch out! There's the Poles-Equator Express!

And there's the poky Trans-Atlantic crawling along the bottom!

CIRCLING SURFACE CURRENTS

For something you can't even see, wind sure can stir things up — from the leaves on a tree to the laundry on your clothesline to a whole ocean! When hot air around the earth's equator rises, cold air from the poles rushes in to take its place, pushing the upper layer of ocean water along with it. Then the earth, rotating on its axis, gets into the act, too, putting its own spin on things. With all this circling around, surface currents continually blend icy water and very warm water. This keeps the earth's temperature suitable (not too cold and not too hot) for humans — and other forms of life — to thrive.

Try This! Fill a mixing bowl almost to the top with water and sprinkle on a pinch of cornmeal. Now blow easily and steadily across the water surface and watch the way the cornmeal is carried by the currents.

The same thing happens when wind blows across the surface of our spinning planet: Ocean waters are swept around by circling currents, steered clockwise in the Northern Hemisphere and counterclockwise in the Southern Hemisphere. This is called the *Coriolis* (CORE-ee-oh-lis) *effect*, named after Gustave Gaspard Coriolis, a French physics professor. In the early 1800s, he was the first person to figure out that the earth's rotation puts a spin on the wind, too.

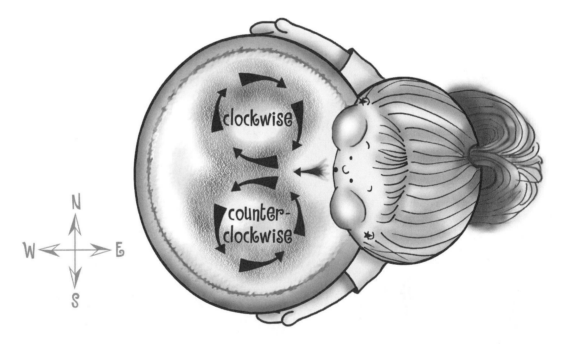

The Coriolis Effect: Note how the cornmeal "currents" swirl clockwise in the Northern Hemisphere and counterclockwise in the Southern Hemisphere.

Awesome Ocean Science!

SPECIAL DELIVERY!

In the spring of 1991, hundreds of brand-new Nike sneakers started showing up on the Oregon (U.S.) coast. Even mermaids don't wear shoes, so where in the world did they come from? Turns out that a year earlier, during a big storm, 80,000 Nikes had washed off the deck of a freighter en route from Korea. From there, the shoes had been picked up by ocean currents and carried for thousands of miles before coming ashore in Oregon! More sneakers turned up on beaches all the way from northern California to Canada as well as in Hawaii, Wake Island, the Philippines, and Japan! Take a look at this map of the major ocean currents in the Pacific and see if you can figure out the route the sneakers took.

CURRENTS VS. WAVES

Currents move water and objects (like Nikes!) across the ocean; waves make the water they're passing through (and whatever is floating on it) rise and fall.

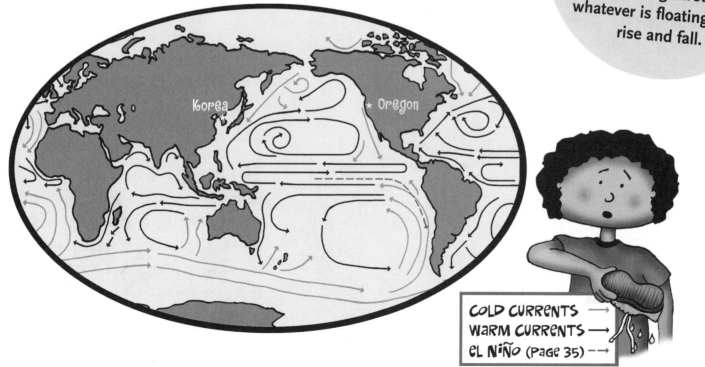

Korea   ★ Oregon

COLD CURRENTS →
WARM CURRENTS →
EL NIÑO (page 35) →

What You Need

- Large baking pan
- Water
- Ruler
- Small ice pack or plastic bag filled with ice cubes
- Food coloring

What You Do

1. Fill the baking pan with an inch (2.5 cm) of room-temperature tap water. Set the ice pack or plastic bag in the water against one end of the pan.

2. Squeeze a drop of food coloring in the water just in front of the ice and another single drop at the opposite end of the pan. Watch carefully and compare what happens to the two drops.

Deep-Water Currents

Deep-water currents aren't warmed by the sun like surface currents. Nor are they directly affected by surface winds. So they tend to travel in straighter lines as they make their way slowly across the oceans.

What's Happening?

Before long, the color from the drop nearest the ice will begin to move steadily forward, forming a long streak. That's because cold water from the melting ice pushes the warmer water, including the food coloring, toward the opposite end of the pan. The drop of coloring that's already at the far end has no place to go because the advancing cold water prevents it from spreading.

Awesome Ocean Science!

All's Well that Upwells

While surface currents regulate ocean temperatures by circulating warm water from the equator and cool water from the poles, deep currents deliver food to ocean life.

Here's how it happens. In places where surface water drifts away, water from the deeper levels flows in, carrying nutrients to large fish populations living in the shallows. The same process — called *upwelling* — happens when the ocean's surface cools down and, therefore, becomes more dense (page 17) than the water below it. As the denser surface water sinks, the water from the bottom rises to replace it.

Try This! First, make a colored ice cube in a small paper cup: Fill the cup halfway, mix in a few drops of food coloring, and freeze it solid. (It's worth the wait!)

When the cube is ready, fill a tall drinking glass almost to the top with luke-warm water. Peel away the paper cup and gently drop the ice cube into the water to cool the surface. In just a few seconds you should see ribbons of color streaming through the water. In what direction are they moving? Can you figure out why?

Wow! Look! My mini ocean is upwelling!

What's Happening?

As the ice cube melts, the coloring catches a ride with the chilled water, which is quick to sink, making way for the warmer, less dense liquid that rises from below to take its place.

Plankton on the Go

Sneakers and messages-in-bottles aren't the only things that get swept along in ocean currents. So do millions of minuscule plants, called *phytoplankton*, and animals, called *zooplankton*. (The word *plankton* is derived from the Greek word for "drifter" or "wanderer.")

Like other plants, phytoplankton convert energy from the sun into food, producing oxygen in a process called *photosynthesis*. Then, the phytoplankton become food for zooplankton as well as for bigger animals that eat both plants *and* animals. As the first link in the *food chain* — the chain of plants and animals linked together because one is a source of food for the next — plankton are essential to the survival of all sea animals. And currents do the very important job of distributing these tiny plants and animals all around

the oceans. Sometimes, fish will turn to face the current and let "plankton soup" flow right into their mouths! How's that for fast food?

Try This! To see how easily tiny sea plants and animals are shuttled around by ocean currents, fill a large wide-mouthed jar almost to the top with water. Vigorously stir the water with a wooden spoon to create a visible whirlpool. Drop buttons, sequins, or other small lightweight items into the jar one by one. The objects will ride the current, spiraling down into the whirl and then circling around and around the bottom of the jar for quite a long while. Looks like fun, doesn't it?

The Case of the Disappearing Anchovy Buffet

If you're an anchovy going out for a bite to eat, the coastal waters of Peru have a great all-you-can-eat buffet that's hard to beat — lots and lots of plankton brought in fresh, courtesy of the cold-water current called the Humboldt or Peruvian Current. The only hitch comes when Humboldt can't make the regular delivery.

Every few years, the trade winds die down that blow from north to south toward the equator and normally direct surface currents offshore from South America's west coast toward the western tropical Pacific. That allows a layer of warm water to flow back toward the Peruvian coast and block the plankton-rich Humboldt from surfacing.

Fishermen who first noticed this current more than 400 years ago named it El Niño — which means "the boy child" in Spanish, and refers to the Christ child — because it shows up around Christmastime.

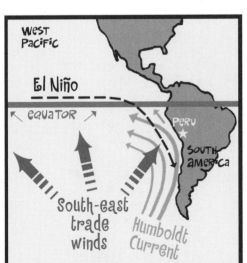

Whenever El Niño arrives, huge schools of anchovies, deprived of the food they're used to, swim off for distant shores. In turn, seals and seabirds that feed on those anchovies are left wanting — not to mention the fishermen who depend on a good catch to make their living.

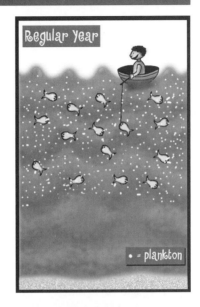

WHAT YOU NEED

- ⚓ 2 wide-mouthed jars that are the same size
- ⚓ Water
- ⚓ Blue and yellow food coloring
- ⚓ Spoon
- ⚓ Large pan or plastic tub (for catching spills)
- ⚓ Index card
- ⚓ A partner

WHAT YOU DO

1. Fill up one jar with very cold water (the Humboldt). Stir in a few drops of blue food coloring. Set the jar in the pan or tub.

2. Fill the second jar to the rim with very warm water (El Niño); color the water yellow. Dip your finger in the water and run it around the rim of the jar. Then place the index card on top of the warm-water jar, gently but firmly pressing it against the rim to create a seal.

What's Happening?

Ta-da! The warm yellow water stays on top, giving the cold blue water no place to go. Except for a thin green layer in the middle, called the *thermocline*, there's virtually no mixing of the two. That's just what happens with El Niño and Humboldt. Eventually, the thermocline will get bigger and bigger until the water in both jars is the same temperature. But, even in your mini ocean, it can take hours! No wonder the anchovies don't hang around.

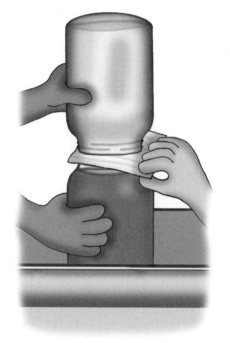

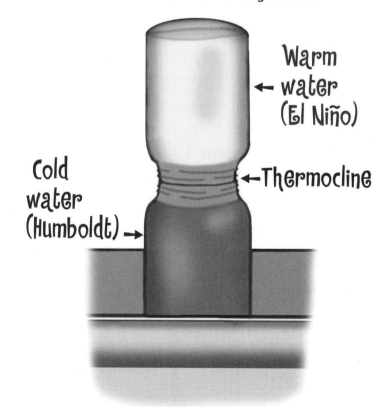

Warm water (El Niño)

←Thermocline

Cold water (Humboldt) →

3. Turn the warm-water jar upside down (go ahead, be brave!) and set it on top of the other bottle so that the two rims are lined up exactly. Now ask a friend to hold both jars steady while you slowly (and carefully!) pull the card out from between them.

Just for fun! What do you think would happen if you repeated this activity putting the cold water on top and the warm water on the bottom? Try it and see if you're right.

Awesome Ocean Science!

CHANGING SCENES: SHORELINES & TIDE POOLS

The shoreline — where water meets land — is as varied as the artists who have tried to capture it on paper or canvas. In some places, the land towers above sea level, forming jagged cliffs or narrower *headlands* (points of land that jut out into the ocean), looking as though they're standing up and holding back the water. Standing on the shore beside one of these puts you in complete awe of nature's power. Humans feel small next to these cliffs.

Other spots, like sandy beaches or marshes, form a more gradual transition between land and sea. Here, instead of chiseling into the land, the sea molds the shore, smoothing out some beaches and building up others. Rocky pools and shallow puddles all along these coastlines are home to some fascinating marine animals — crusty barnacles, knobby sea cucumbers, prickly urchins, and many more. We feel as if we are on a movie set when we enter this curious, still world, with its hidden surprises. Yes, the shoreline holds many secrets.

Shaping Shores

Q: What is soft as cotton and as sharp as a knife?

A: Water!

Water is so soft you can wash your face with it, yet it's super-strong, too — strong enough to carve through rock, forming craggy cliffs! How does the water do that? As ocean waves break against the coast, they push air into tiny cracks in the rocky shoreline with enough force to crumble soil and split rock! Eventually, the outer bank — and whatever may be built on top of it — *erodes* (is worn away), and the ocean moves farther in.

Water-carved coastline, Algarve, Portugal

WHO SHOULD PAY?

You've probably seen it on TV many times: Hurricane winds combined with high tide send huge waves crashing into the cliffs where fancy resorts sit atop beautiful coastlines. And then it happens: A million-dollar home where the owners had enjoyed spectacular ocean views is perched atop a cliff that suddenly breaks loose. The house topples to the ocean floor.

Who should pay? The government's emergency funds (FEMA)? The insurance company? Well, how about the owners who should have known what you know — that the force of water can cause even the mightiest cliffs to crumble? What do you think, Ambassador of the Ocean?

WHERE DOES BEACH SAND COME FROM, ANYWAY?

When rocks and minerals get knocked around, the way they do when the surf surges in and out, tiny bits are ground off. These grains can be jet black, like the lava sands of Hawaii, or snow white, like the crushed shell and coral beaches of the Caribbean Islands. Some beaches are even pink, such as on the island of Eleuthera, in the Bahamas. (What do you think *that* sand is made from?) Mostly, sand is a beige or tan blend of quartz rock and other materials such as feldspar, mica, magnetite, and garnet. Whatever kind it is, it's fun to play with, that's for sure!

"My Beach is Younger than Yours!"

Q: How do you tell an old beach from a new one?

A: Well, an old beach is bigger *and* smaller.

Huh? How's that for a confusing answer? Over time, as waves continually carry new material ashore, a beach generally grows wider while, at the same time, the individual grains of sand are ground finer and finer. Sometimes though, when a beach has built up into a steep slope, the waves will start washing sand back out to sea. It's almost as though the ocean keeps tabs and makes sure each shore has just the right amount.

OK, GUYS. THAT'S ENOUGH SAND. HEAD DOWN TO THE SOUTH, PLEASE.

WHAT YOU NEED

- ⚓ Large baking pan
- ⚓ Clean sand (the kind you fill sandboxes with)
- ⚓ Water
- ⚓ Spatula or ruler

WHAT YOU DO

1. Set the pan on a level surface and fill one-third of it with sand. Shape the sand into a steep, loosely packed slope at one end. Then, gently pour water into the other end of the pan until the level reaches halfway up your sandy beach.

2. Use the edge of the spatula or ruler to gently and steadily push waves of water toward the sand. Don't go too fast — wait for one wave to bounce back before sending off the next one, just as the ocean does. After a few minutes, what do you notice about the slope of the sand both above and below the *watermark* (the water level on the sand)? Where is the watermark now?

Notice how the incoming waves had to go uphill while the outgoing ones had a quick run downhill. This creates an *undertow*, a current traveling in the opposite direction from the surface current. Strong undertows can quickly carry sand back out to sea, smoothing the beach into a much gentler slope in the process. (They can carry swimmers out also, so you need to be especially careful if you're swimming where the undertow is strong.)

3. Now that you've seen how the ocean reshapes a steep beach, can you predict what it will do to a relatively flat one? Pour out the water and remold the sand to be flatter. Then, add enough new water to cover two-thirds of the beach — and bring on the waves!

What's Happening?

On a flat beach, outgoing waves don't create as strong an undertow as those flowing down a steeply sloped beach. So sand that's carried ashore by those waves tends to settle on top of the beach and build up, instead of being swept right back out to sea.

Rub a few grains of sand between your fingers. Are they soft and powdery or hard and coarse? The finer the beach sand is, the more tightly the grains will pack together, making it harder for ocean waves to sink in. That's why fine sand generally shapes into a smooth, solid, gently sloped beach. Coarse sand tends to pile loosely, creating plenty of small air pockets for water to get in and move things around. What shape do you think a beach with coarse sand is likely to take?

The Tow on Your Toes!

The next time you are at the beach, see if you can feel an undertow. Standing right at the waterline, notice what happens when the water rushes in and rushes out almost at the same moment. Do you feel your feet sinking as the sand is towed out from under your toes?

Tidal Tidings

Waves, currents, wind, and humans, too — there sure are plenty of forces shaping the shore. And the one that's probably the most important of all is farthest away. In fact, it's in outer space! You guessed it — it's the moon. As it circles around our planet, it acts like a dance partner swinging and spinning the ocean toward and back from the shore.

Awesome Ocean Science!

The Battle of the Bulge

You could say there's a tug-of-war going on to win the ocean. First and foremost, earth's gravity (the force that attracts things toward it — as a magnet does) is constantly pulling the ocean toward the planet's center, or core. Otherwise, the earth's water might just spin off into space! But the moon (and the sun, too, to a lesser extent because it's farther away) tugs the ocean away from the earth. This causes the water to bulge up on whichever side of the planet is facing the moon at the time. Makes sense so far, right? But how do you explain this: At the same time that the part of the ocean nearest the moon forms a bulge, so does the water on the opposite side of the earth. It's almost as if the ocean is trying to divide itself in two. Want to see what's happening?

WHAT YOU NEED

- ⚓ Paper circle, 2" (5 cm) in diameter
- ⚓ Corrugated cardboard
- ⚓ Pipe cleaner
- ⚓ String
- ⚓ Pushpin

WHAT YOU DO

1. Center the paper circle (this will be the earth's crust-covered core) on the cardboard. Shape the pipe cleaner into a ring and tie the string to it. Place the ring on the cardboard so that it completely circles the core (the ring represents the surface of the world's oceans). Press the pushpin into the cardboard *between* the ring and the circle, opposite the point where the string is attached.

SURFACE OF OCEAN

YOU (MOON)

2. Now you're ready to play the part of the moon. Gently but steadily pull on the string. See the ring bulge toward you? Like the pipe cleaner, the real ocean is flexible. Because it's a fluid, it can change its shape when it's tugged. But the earth's gravity (like the pushpin here) prevents the ocean from being pulled completely away from the earth's core.

3. But wait, your job's not over yet! The moon's gravity pulls on the earth's core as well as on the oceans floating on top of the earth's crust. So go ahead, move the paper circle a little closer to you, and presto! There's the bulge on the opposite side of the earth.

One more thing! The earth itself also plays a role in building up that bulge on the side opposite the moon. When an object moves in a circle or a curved path, its *matter* (the substance it's made up of) gets pulled outward away from the center. This pulling is called *centrifugal force*. So when our planet circles the sun, the ocean gets pulled away from the earth's core by centrifugal force. If you've ever been pressed against your seat on a spinning amusement ride, then you've experienced centrifugal force, too!

What's Happening?

Have you figured out why the earth's core doesn't change shape as much as the oceans? Compared with the fluid in the ocean, the core of the earth is rather rigid — so it takes more force to change its shape. That's why the effects of the moon's gravitational pull are less visible on the body of the earth than on its oceans.

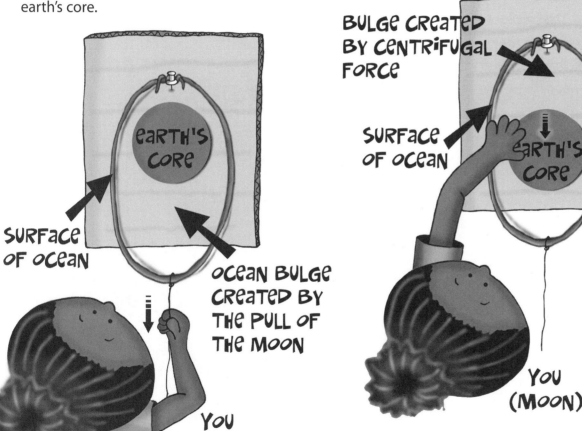

SURFACE OF OCEAN

EARTH'S CORE

OCEAN BULGE CREATED BY THE PULL OF THE MOON

YOU (MOON)

BULGE CREATED BY CENTRIFUGAL FORCE

SURFACE OF OCEAN

EARTH'S CORE

YOU (MOON)

Awesome Ocean Science!

THE SECRET'S OUT: TURNING TIDES

So, now you know the secret of the ocean's tides. Throughout the day, as the earth turns on its axis, different parts of the ocean are pulled toward the moon. In the open ocean you're not likely to notice a thing, but along a shoreline, you can actually see the water rise up and cover more of the land. It's called *high tide*. At the same time, those places on earth where the water has been pulled away experience *low tides*.

Just how high a tide rises depends on the slope and size of the land. In the long, narrow Bay of Fundy in Nova Scotia, Canada, the water rises some 53' (16 m) between low and high tides! The next time your family goes to an ocean beach, spend some time noticing how far up the shore the breaking waves come each time. Can you tell whether the tide is coming in or going out?

Let's see ... I'll go to the beach around 8:30 today to collect shells!

WELLFLEET TIDE CHART

Day	High Tide am	PM	Low Tide am	PM
SUN.	12:56	12:59		
MON.	1:40	1:44	6:52	7:28
TUES.	2:27	2:34	7:38	8:14
WED.	3:16	3:07	8:27	9:03
RS.	4:09		9:21	9:54
SAT.	5:05		10:18	10:48
UN.	6:01		11:19	11:44
.	6:59		11:59	12:21
	7:55		12:42	1:23
			1:40	2:23

Tide's Out!

With soft, warm sand underfoot, refreshing surf beckoning you to dive in and cool off, and a breathtaking view, the beach sure is a nice place to visit on a hot summer's day. But, as the saying goes, you wouldn't want to live there. Life in the *intertidal zone* (between the high and low tide marks), where the ocean can leave you high and dry for hours, then return to douse you with pounding waves, comes up short on all the creature comforts we humans enjoy so much. No matter, as there are plenty of creatures that happily call it home!

Neighborhoods of marine animals and plants have special ways of coping with the daily extremes of life at the edge of the sea.

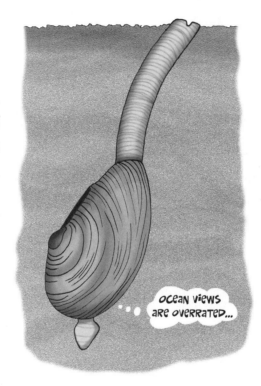

ocean views are overrated...

Lichen (LI-ken), a bushlike plant produced by fungi and algae, grows low to the ground just above the high-tide mark, where it won't catch as much wind. *Limpets* and *mussels* (types of shellfish) attach themselves to rocks near the low-tide line, where they filter plankton and algae from the water that washes over them. And *crabs*, the ultimate scavengers, follow the tide ashore, scooting along sideways as they snatch stranded shrimp and mussels and clean up the remains of other marine animals.

UNDERGROUND DIGS

A variety of animals, such as *clams* and *cockles* (shellfish), set up residence right on the beach by burrowing into the soft sand or mud above the low-tide line. (So much for enjoying a great ocean view!) Still, living underground offers some considerable pluses, like shelter from the pounding waves, predators, and the hot sun (or bitter cold). Other creatures, like *mussels* and *sponges*, secrete fluids that dissolve limestone to create hollows they can move into. And the *sea urchin*, looking like a mini porcupine, can even use its prickly spines to chisel out a home in solid rock! The one hitch: If its little cave is too snug a fit, a growing sea urchin can get stuck inside!

Awesome Ocean Science!

Rocky Residences

Mini–saltwater ponds called *tide pools*, most often found along rocky coastlines, are often teeming with a variety of fascinating sea creatures. If you have a chance to check out some tide pools, be sure to coordinate your adventure with low tide, when the water will be shallow enough to find them (check for the tide charts in the local newspaper). And wear sneakers or shoes — a rocky shore can be slippery and sharp!

Remember to observe the animals in their natural environment, using a handy tide-pool viewer. Please don't remove the creatures from the tide pool. Guaranteed, they will die away from their natural habitat. (Many aquariums have re-created tide pools where you can also observe these critters.)

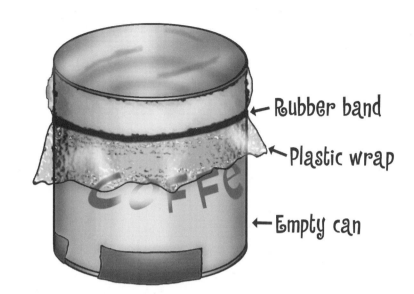

← Rubber band

← Plastic wrap

← Empty can

Try This! Use a can opener to remove the top and bottom of a large empty can; carefully cover any sharp edges with duct tape. Stretch plastic wrap across the can's top, using a wide rubber band to secure it in place. Now gently pull on the sides of the plastic to create a tight seal and a smooth surface. Your viewer is ready to be used! Just lower the plastic-wrapped end into the water and enjoy a clear view of whatever lies below the surface!

Tide-Pool Etiquette

IT'S COOL TO BE CALM: When you're looking for signs of life in a tide pool, at first glance you may think there's nothing to see. But remember, these are shy creatures — their survival depends greatly on not being detected by predators! Wait, sit still, and keep an eye peeled. Without warning, something that looked like a rock an instant ago just may start swimming! Or you might suddenly notice a skinny pipefish swimming upright to blend in with strands of eelgrass.

GENTLE DOES IT: If you want to see what's under a rock, turn it over very gently. Once you've checked things out, replace the rock. (Imagine if a curious, friendly giant lifted up your house to see inside but didn't bother to put it back before he left. You'd be without a home!)

LOOK BUT DON'T TAKE: Remember, tide-pool creatures belong in a tide pool. So, as fascinating as they may be, that's where you should leave them — first, because they won't survive elsewhere, and second, because many tide-pool residents, such as sea stars and sea urchins, are equipped with spines that can poke or sting you.

JUST FOR FUN!

No need for step-by-step instructions — just bring along your creativity, crafting odds and ends, toothpicks, pipe cleaners, and some good illustrations of sea creatures. Then, go to it, and make a tide pool full of critters. Enjoy!

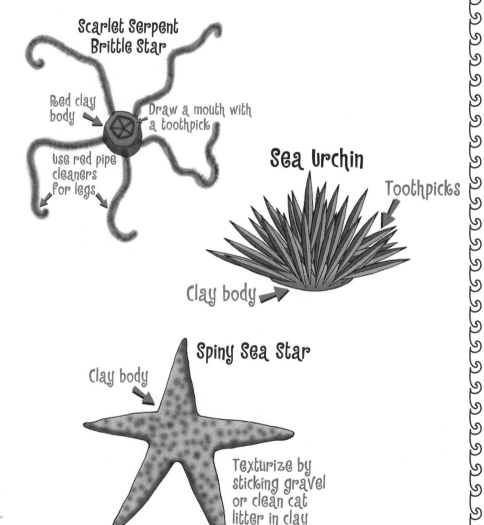

Scarlet Serpent Brittle Star

Red clay body

Draw a mouth with a toothpick

Use red pipe cleaners for legs

Sea Urchin

Toothpicks

Clay body

Spiny Sea Star

Clay body

Texturize by sticking gravel or clean cat litter in clay

Salty Characters

The kinds of animals you'll find in a particular tide pool depend on the area's climate and the pool's proximity to the ocean. So, you might want to pick up a good guidebook ahead of time to help you identify them. One thing *all* tide-pool residents have in common, though, is their amazing ability to deal with the drastic changes in their environment that occur several times every day. When the tide is out and the pool gets really warm and salty (or starts to dry up!), the critters move under rocks and seaweed to keep their bodies moist. Then, when the tide flows back in, they come out of hiding to collect their share of the fresh oxygen and food the water carries in. Here's a sampling of tide-pool residents you're likely to encounter:

Barnacles can look like white, tan, or black paint spattered against dark rock walls, but they are living creatures. With a little luck, you can watch them feed: As the ocean flows over them, crusty valves open and feathery feet pop up, kicking plankton into their bodies every few seconds.

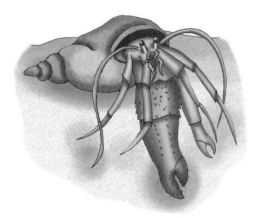

Hermit crabs aren't the least bit shy about making themselves right at home. To protect its soft abdomen, this crab moves into another creature's shell — sometimes pulling out the former resident first! If you notice a head and claws poking out of a snail shell, you've probably discovered a hermit crab. They are quite the characters to watch!

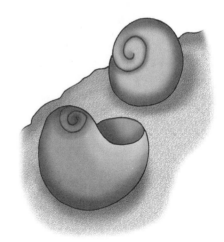

Periwinkles, often abundant in tide pools, are hard-shelled snails that vary in color. You'll probably find them in clusters, grazing on algae-coated rocks.

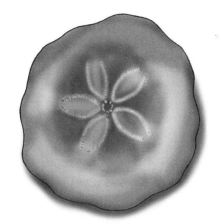

Sand dollars often line the bottom of a tide pool, making it resemble a wishing well. The center of each little disc is adorned with a star-shaped imprint. To weigh themselves down, young sand dollars swallow grains of sand!

Sea cucumbers, which eat scraps of plants and animals, are sometimes found burrowed in the sand. Although their color ranges from gray to rose, you'll probably recognize the knobby oblong shape that gives them their name.

It's a Test!

Live sand dollars are covered with short, tiny spines — much like fur — that range in color from gray to purple to greenish brown. The smooth, bleached-white shells (the external skeletons) of dead sand dollars that often wash up on the beach are called tests. (And this is one test you'll be happy to take!)

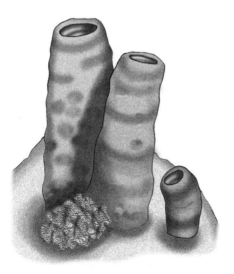

Sponges, many of which protrude like fingers from the floor and walls of tide pools, actually are large colonies of minuscule creatures. These animals eat by sifting food from the water as it flows through the many holes in their bodies.

Awesome Ocean Science!

SECRETS OF THE DEEP: THE OCEAN FLOOR

For centuries, sailors crossed the oceans but never had a clue what lay below them on the ocean floor. Sure, they reported seeing all kinds of marine animals cruising through the water, but most people believed the deep seafloor was nothing more than an empty plain where no life could survive. After all, it was dark and cold, with tremendous water pressure pushing down. Well, it turns out the ocean bed is far from empty — or flat! Thanks to modern submersible exploration vehicles, we've learned that the seafloor is covered with all kinds of mountains, volcanoes,

canyons, and even waterfalls — many of which make the ones on land look small. Plus, all kinds of unusual creatures, including giant worms (how about one 4'/1.2 m long!) and enormous clams, make themselves right at home in the deepest, darkest, coldest depths. Even so, scientists still know much less about the ocean floor than they do about the surface of the moon! Isn't that surprising? The good news is there's plenty left for *you* to discover!

So get on board for an amazing underwater voyage where you can learn all about some of the deep sea's long-kept secrets.

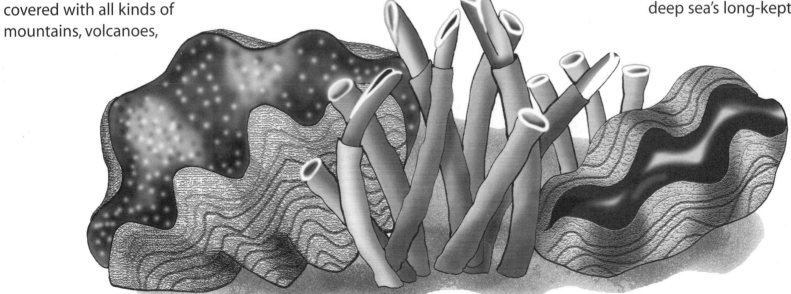

Our Final Frontier

It may be hard to believe but scientists had spotted the rings of Saturn and the moons around Jupiter hundreds of years before anyone had an inkling of what may lie at the bottom of our very own oceans! The telescope had been invented in the 1600s, but it wasn't until 1872 that Sir Charles Wyville Thomson, a Scottish professor, led the first true ocean voyage of exploration aboard the HMS (Her Magesty's Ship) *Challenger*. During the four-year, 69,000-mile (111,021 km) expedition, the crew scooped and scraped samples of water and seafloor from 362 ocean stations around the world. In the process, they discovered long mountain chains and hundreds of animals that had never been seen before! The exploration certainly changed people's belief that the ocean floor was flat and lifeless.

Drawing of the HMS *Challenger*

Can You Fathom That?

At the time the ocean ship Challenger *set sail, ocean depth was measured through a method called* sounding: *A weighted rope that was knotted or otherwise marked every 6' (1.8 m) was lowered overboard. When it reached the bottom, the sea level line was marked on the rope. As the rope was pulled back in, the intervals between knots, called* fathoms, *were counted up. The greatest measurement recorded during the expedition, 26,850' (8,262 m), was taken in the Pacific between the Philippines and Guam. Now we know the ship was over the Mariana Trench, which is still the deepest place known on earth! In fact, parts of it are even deeper than the* Challenger *crew ever imagined.*

In 1960, a two-person cast-iron submersible vessel called the Trieste *dove 35,802' (11,016 m) — that's nearly 7 miles (11 km)! — into the Trench's very lowest point. Just think, if you were to lower Mount Everest into that very spot (which scientists have aptly named the Challenger Deep), the peak would still be more than a mile (1.6 km) below sea level! Whoa!*

WHAT YOU NEED

- String or yarn, about 14" (35 cm)
- Ruler
- Metal washer (or another small object you can use as a weight)
- Scissors
- Plastic drinking straw
- Rubber band
- Plastic bottle cap
- Paper clip
- Large bowl of water
- 2 or 3 pennies

WHAT YOU DO

1. Make a sounding line by tying knots in the string, spacing them 1" (2.5 cm) apart. To make a weight, tie the washer to the string at the same level as the bottom knot.

2. Cut a small section from the drinking straw; use the rubber band to hold it in place against the side of the bottle cap (your mini ship). Thread the top of the sounding line through the straw and tie the line's end to a paper clip so it won't pull back through.

3. Holding onto the paper clip, set the ship afloat in the bowl. If the cap seems tippy, add cargo (a few pennies) to weight it down a bit. Let the washer come to rest on the bottom of the bowl while keeping the line straight. How many inches (cm) deep is your ocean?

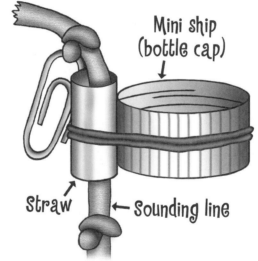

Mini ship (bottle cap)

Straw ← Sounding line

4. Now blow across the water surface to stir up an ocean breeze. As your ship drifts, watch what happens to your sounding line. Can you see how certain conditions, such as weather and currents, may have affected the accuracy of some readings?

BOUNCING SOUND

Only in the last few decades, with the use of modern submersibles (small underwater vehicles) and unmanned *remote-operated vehicles* (ROVs), have scientists begun to compile more precise measurements of ocean depth. Instead of using sounding lines, these vehicles use *sonar*: They transmit *sound waves*, or pings, through the water, timing how long it takes for the pings to bounce, or echo, back from the seafloor. That time is all they need to figure out the depth at that location. The funny thing is, toothed whales (and bats above ground) have been using sound in the same way (a process you may have heard of called *echolocation*) to familiarize themselves with their surroundings long before we humans ever thought of it!

Here's how sonar works: Suppose it takes eight seconds for a sound wave to travel to the ocean floor and back. Divide that time in half to get the time it takes for a one-way trip to the bottom. Multiply your answer by the speed of sound in water, which is 4,800' (1,477 m) per second. The distance to the ocean floor is 19,200' (5,907 m)!

> **8 seconds ÷ 2 = 4 seconds**
> **for sound to travel from the surface to the ocean floor**
> **4 x 4,800' (1,477 m) = 19,200' (5,907 m)**

Sound waves

Echo

Try This! Hold a metal pie plate on edge. Place your wristwatch (it needs to be the kind that makes a ticking noise) in the end of a paper-towel tube; have a friend hold the tube so that the empty end is close to but not touching the pie plate. Hold a second paper-towel tube with one end near the pie plate so that it forms a 45° angle with the first tube. Listen through the opposite end of the second tube. You should be able to hear the distinct ticking of the watch.

Can you figure out why the sound waves traveling through the first tube change direction and head up the second tube?

What's Happening?

Think of each tick of your watch as a ping of sonar. The sound waves travel straight through the paper-towel tube your watch is in until they reach the pie plate. There, the waves bounce off the solid metal surface (just as sonar bounces off the ocean floor) and travel back through the second tube to your ear.

MAPPING THE OCEAN FLOOR

Nowadays, ships tow echo-sounders called *bathyscans* that send out as many as 120 sound waves at once! The results of all these echo soundings are calculated, compiled, and translated by computers into detailed images of the ocean floor. Commercial fishermen use echolocation to locate fish, too, so they'll know the best place to set their lines.

Manned Submersibles & ROV-ing Wonders!

Thanks to the invention of manned submersibles (small, free-moving, underwater vehicles) and ROVs (remote-operated vehicles), scientists have finally been able to explore, photograph, and map out some of the very deepest sections of the ocean floor.

- The *TRIESTE,* a small two-person cast-iron submersible, holds the record (set in 1960) for the deepest dive ever — 35,802' (11,016 m) — into the Mariana Trench in the Pacific Ocean.

- More maneuverable than the *Trieste*, the *ALVIN*, a three-person submersible, dives as deep as 14,764' (4,543 m). Not only can it navigate through and hover in rugged underwater terrain, sometimes it even rests right on the ocean floor.

During the last four decades, the *Alvin* has been used for several thousand explorations, allowing scientists to survey such sights as deep-sea vents and the sunken *Titanic!*

- The *ARGO*, an unmanned sledlike ROV, towed behind a research ship at the ocean surface, takes soundings and photographs at depths down to 19,684' (6,057 m).

- *JASON*, a small robot equipped with TV cameras and lights is tethered to submersibles such as the *Alvin* and sent by remote control into places that are too small or difficult for other vehicles to explore.

The *Trieste II* submersible

Awesome Ocean Science!

Revolving Floor

The Andes mountains, stretching 4,500 miles (7,240 km) through seven South American countries (Argentina, Chile, Bolivia, Peru, Ecuador, Colombia, and Venezuela), form the longest mountain chain on any continent. But the longest range on earth is actually underwater! Spanning from the Arctic Ocean through the Atlantic, then into the Indian and Pacific oceans, the *Mid-Ocean Ridge is seven times longer than the Andes range!* Here, and at other under-sea ridges, new ocean crust forms. Lava oozes out of the *rift* (a deep crack along the center of the ridge) and pushes old crust to either side as it cools and solidifies. With the seafloor continually spreading like that, you may think the earth would get wider and wider, but it doesn't. At the same time new crust is formed, the far edges of older crust slide into deep-sea trenches (a process called *subduction*) and melt back into the earth's *mantle* (page 11). The western coast of South America slides over the edge of the Pacific, while the edge of the Pacific melts back into the center of the earth. That's why the Atlantic Ocean continues to grow wider as the Pacific slowly gets narrower. Now that's some recycling act!

WELCOME TO THE MID-OCEAN RIDGE TRAIL

57

Aloha! Hawaii

Lava actually rises through thousands of cracks and holes, called *hot spots*, in the earth's crust. In time, some of these undersea volcanoes build up higher than sea level. That's just how the Hawaiian Islands were created. Lava percolating up from a hot spot below the Pacific formed one island after another, creating a chain, as the oceanic plate continued to slide over it. In fact, it's still happening. The newest volcano in the chain, Loihi, is still under water, but scientists expect it to eventually break the surface — in several tens of thousands of years!

Try This! Pour 1 tablespoon (15 ml) of vegetable oil into the bottom of a tall drinking glass. Cover the oil with 2 tablespoons (30 ml) of salt. Fill the glass with water and wait a minute or so. As the salt dissolves, it's no longer heavy enough to hold down the oil. Just like lava punching through the oceanic crust, blobs of oil will burst through the layer of dissolving salt and rise through the water.

Island Shores

Not all islands started out as volcanoes, though — some are actually extensions of the continents they're near. The British Isles (the two islands with England, Scotland, Wales, and Ireland, plus thousands of smaller ones) for instance, were part of the European mainland until glacial melt from the last ice age poured into the lower spaces between them. There are barrier islands, too, like Hatteras and Ocracoke and the other islands that form the Outer Banks of North Carolina along the East Coast of the U.S. They're created when gravel or silt slides from the mainland and piles up offshore.

Awesome Ocean Science!

swallowed by the sea?

The lost city of *Atlantis* is said to have been swallowed by the sea. Was it a real place or the setting of a myth? For more than 2,000 years, since the Greek philosopher Plato wrote about this intriguing empire, that question has been debated but never answered. Hear the story and decide for yourself:

More than 11,000 years ago, an island in the middle of the Atlantic Ocean called Atlantis belonged to Poseidon, the Greek god of the sea. Poseidon fell in love with a woman named Cleito and together they raised five sets of twin boys. Thus, Poseidon divided his empire on Atlantis into 10 sections, each to be ruled by one of his sons. People loved living in Atlantis! The soil was so rich, they could grow all kinds of herbs, fruits, and nuts. It wasn't long before the island became a big center of trade and the people there became quite rich. But some-times, as it is said, the more you have, the more you want. And so it went — the people of Atlantis who had so much became quite greedy and dishonest. Surely this didn't set very well with the other gods! They decided to put a quick end to it all by starting a violent earthquake that set giant waves in motion. The ocean washed over the 10 sections of land and the island of Atlantis sank instantly, never to be seen again!

Or maybe not? On December 4, 2000, while exploring the ocean floor in a submersible vessel (page 56), oceanographers Donna Blackman, Deborah Kelley, and Jeff Karson discovered about two dozen gleaming white stone towers rising as high as 18-story buildings. They were unlike any other underwater formations found before, and they also just happen to be located on a seafloor mountain named Atlantis Massif, which prompted the scientists to name their finding The Lost City.

Still, scientists favor another explanation of how these curious towers came to be constructed. In this region, seawater flowing down through cracks in the ocean floor comes in contact with a glassy green rock called *olivine*. When it does, things heat up, and the olivine is transformed into a mineral called *serpentine*, which piles up into grand mounds and towers.

Hmmm. Which explanation do you agree with?

The Force Is With You

Q: What has about 15 pounds (7 kg) of pressure on its body and doesn't feel it?

A: *You* do!

Every minute of the day, in most places on earth, air presses against every square inch (cm) of your body with nearly 15 pounds (7 kg) of force — or, as scientists call it, *one atmosphere*. The pressure is equally distributed throughout your body, so you don't feel a thing. You only notice when the air pressure changes, such as when you're riding in a car up a really steep hill and your ears get blocked.

In the ocean, changes in pressure are more noticeable. That's because water is much denser (page 17) than air. Here's the scoop: For every 33' (10 m) that you go down in the ocean underwater, the pressure increases by one more atmosphere. If you were able to reach the bottom of the Mariana Trench (page 52), your body would be under so much pressure, it'd be like trying to stand up under the weight of several dozen jumbo jets!

33' (10 m) underwater = 1 atmosphere of pressure

Try This! Fill a large bowl or wide-mouthed jar halfway with water. Pull a plastic bread bag up over your hand and wrist; use a rubber band to seal the top around your forearm. Dunk your hand into the water and you'll discover that, even in a mere bowlful, there's enough water pressure to make you feel as though your hand's been shrink-wrapped!

I've been shrink-wrapped!

Try This! Using a pushpin or a large needle, make a vertical row of four holes in the side of a large empty plastic soda bottle. Start about 1" (2.5 cm) from the bottom and space the holes about 1" (2.5 cm) apart. Fill the bottle with tap water and set it down in the sink. Can you see how the angle and force of each stream is affected by the volume (amount) of water above it?

What's Happening?

Notice how the water squirting out of the lowest hole makes the straightest stream? That's because it's under the greatest pressure — the weight of all the water above that hole pushes down on it. The stream coming out of the top hole has the least weight pressing on it, so it's the most droopy.

Hard-Pressed

Human beings have walked across beds of nails, tightropes, and even the surface of the moon! But one place human beings have yet to trek is on the deep seafloor. Don't hold your breath waiting for it to happen, though! Our lungs aren't strong enough to fill with air under the incredible pressure there. But other mammals, such as Weddell seals and whales, are much better at handling the extremes of the deep sea. Rather than fight the pressure, their bodies give in to it by storing more oxygen in their muscles and by allowing their lungs to collapse. Without air in their lungs, these animals become heavier, which also makes it easier for them to glide to great depths where they fish for food.

Try This! Fill a tall glass almost to the top with water. Insert a drinking straw about 1" (2.5 cm) into the water and slowly blow a bubble. It's pretty easy, right? Now, insert the straw farther into the glass so that the end is just 1" (2.5 cm) from the bottom. Again, slowly blow a bubble. Why do you think this takes so much more effort than the first bubble? The same type of pressure that's at work here is what makes it harder and harder to keep your lungs filled with air the deeper underwater you go.

But Is It Art?

A trip to the ocean just wouldn't be complete without bringing home a pretty shell (one that's no longer occupied by an ocean animal, of course!), a smooth piece of sea glass, or another treasure from the sea. Even oceanographers doing research far offshore collect souvenirs. In fact, they have a cool trick for making their own. They decorate plain white Styrofoam cups with drawings or slogans and then lower them way, way down into the deep sea. There, where the water pressure is thousands of pounds (kg) per square inch (cm), the air gets squeezed right out of the Styrofoam! By the time the cups are hauled back aboard, they've shrunk to about the size of a thimble!

COOL! LOOK WHAT I FOUND!

The Bends

Before ocean explorer Jacques-Yves Cousteau and engineer Emile Gagnan invented the *Aqua-Lung* in 1943, divers had to take underwater exploration one step at a time — literally! Wearing metal helmets and heavy, cumbersome suits linked by a cable to the diving boat, divers had little flexibility as they walked along the sea floor. *Scuba* (Self-Contained Underwater Breathing Apparatus) equipment made it possible for divers, for the first time, to swim freely underwater like the fish and other marine animals they hoped to see and study — at least in depths no deeper than 200' (61 m), that is! Below that, the water pressure is just too great.

Even after swimming at safe depths, water pressure can cause a diver to experience a painful condition called *decompression sickness* if she surfaces too quickly. The reason this happens is that when a diver breathes compressed air from the tank, nitrogen (a gas that makes up 80 percent of the air we breathe) gets stored in the blood. Then, when the diver rises, that nitrogen is under increasingly less pressure (remember, water presses harder and harder against your body the deeper you go), so it expands and forms bubbles that can block the flow of blood. Because these bubbles are especially uncomfortable when they form in the bones and joints, decompression sickness is also called *the bends*. If the condition isn't treated in time, it can harm organs and even lead to death.

Deep Sea Life

In 1977, the submersible research vehicle, *Alvin*, made a discovery that changed the age-old belief that all life on earth depended on the sun's energy to make food in the process called photosynthesis. Traveling along the ocean floor near the Galápagos Islands in the Pacific Ocean, *Alvin* came upon a field of underwater hot springs (places in the ocean floor where hot water comes bubbling up, called *hydrothermal vents*). Amazingly, sea animals were thriving in these springs without ever seeing the light of day — not a single ray! Turns out that at some places on the ocean floor, water seeps down into cracks in the earth's crust, eventually reaching the inner layer of *magma* (molten rock). There it heats up to 1,100°F (593°C) and, like a whistling teakettle, blasts back up and out of the vents, bringing a dark mix of metals and chemicals with it. Some of the metals rain down and pile up around the openings, forming chimney-like stacks called *black smokers*. And some of the chemicals are used by bacteria to make food, a process called *chemosynthesis* that feeds the communities of giant clams, worms, and other unusual animals living around the vents. Since this discovery, many scientists believe that life on earth may have started at hydrothermal vents!

Launching the *Alvin*

The *Alvin* at work underwater

Awesome Ocean Science!

Try This! Set off your own hot-water vent! Fill a tall jar almost to the top with very cold water. Stretch the neck of a small balloon and drop in a few pennies for weight. Next, squirt three drops each of red and green food coloring into the balloon. Finally, fill the balloon with very warm tap water — just enough to give it shape without stretching it (as you would a water balloon). Holding the balloon with the very top of the neck pinched closed, gently set it on the floor of the water-filled jar.

Let go, and watch! A column of black water will stream out of the balloon just as water heated by the inner earth flows up through a black smoker into the cold water surrounding it. If you watch long enough, you should see distinct blobs of color start to sink back down, just like the metals that rain back down on the smokers.

Name That Vent

Scientists do a lot of difficult work, but they know how to have fun, too. Witness the names of some of the hundreds of hydrothermal vent fields that have been discovered around the world (the largest one measuring as big as a football field). The ones first found near the Galápagos were dubbed Rose Garden (named after the giant red tube worms living there), Garden of Eden, and East of Eden! Others along the Mid-Atlantic Ridge have names straight out of the American West, such as Broken Spur (where the ridge is covered with spiky points) and Snake Pit (a haven for white, eel-like fish). Particularly popular among scientists was a large black smoker called Godzilla located in a vent field 200 miles (322 km) from Vancouver Island. Godzilla rose about 160' (48 m) — that's as tall as a 15-story building! — and resembled a giant layered mushroom, before it collapsed under its own weight.

AND WHAT ABOUT THOSE GIANT TUBE WORMS?

Unlike earthworms that tunnel through the ground, tube worms stay put, living in protective cylinders that look like giant candlesticks stuck in the ocean floor around hydrothermal vents. Only the bright red tips of their bodies poke out of the tube tops. And even though tube worms never eat — they don't even have a mouth, a stomach, or a digestive system! — they can grow as long as 4' (1.2 m). How do they do it? Instead of food, they depend on bacteria (*symbionts*) living in their bodies for nutrition. These bacteria transform oxygen, sulfide, and other chemicals the worms absorb from the vent water into nourishment to feed both themselves and the tube worms. Now that's what you call an extra-value meal!

 ## Who Turned on the Lights?

In other parts of the deep ocean where no hydrothermal vents are found, it's as frosty cold and pitch black as a closed refrigerator — except there's not much food in it! It can be pretty slim pickings for hungry fish. That's why most deep-sea residents are equipped with a special trait that helps them find prey. It's called bioluminescence, *the ability to make their own light. The angler fish, for example, can light up the end of a fishpole-like fin that hangs in front of its mouth — perfect for luring an unsuspecting meal! Other creatures use bioluminescence to disguise themselves from predators, particularly when their pursuit of food takes them into higher levels where there's scattered light. By regulating their own light, they can match the glow of the sunlight and blend right in.*

WHAT YOU NEED

- ⚓ Empty rectangular tissue box
- ⚓ Thin nail or pushpin
- ⚓ Scissors
- ⚓ Colored paper
- ⚓ Ruler
- ⚓ Thread

WHAT YOU DO

1. Use the nail or pushpin to poke a single peep hole centered in one end panel of the tissue box. Poke a bunch of holes in the opposite end panel.

Here, fishy fishy fishy...

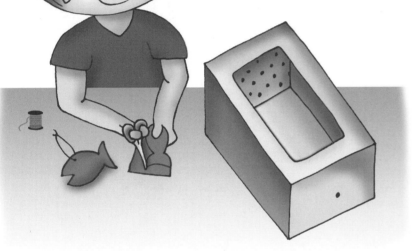

2. From the colored paper, cut out two identical fish shapes about 2" (5 cm) long and 1" (2.5 cm) wide. Poke a dozen or so holes in one fish. Then, loop a piece of thread through a hole at the top of each fish and knot the ends together.

4. Point the box toward a window or light and look through the peep hole. You should clearly see the silhouette of the fish — just as ocean predators spot their prey swimming in shallow sunlit water. Now replace the fish with the one full of holes. This time, all you'll see are pinpoints of twinkling lights — no distinct fish shape! By emitting light of their own, fishes with bioluminescence camouflage themselves in mid-ocean depths where there's scattered light.

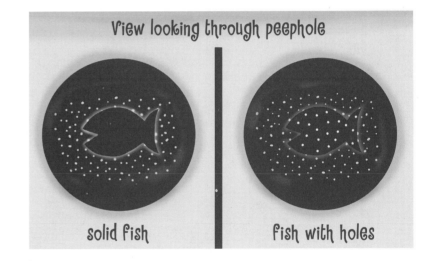

View looking through peephole

solid fish   fish with holes

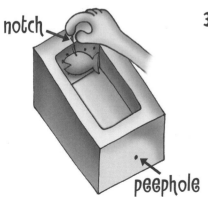

notch

peephole

3. Hang the fish without holes inside the box in front of the panel with multiple holes. To do this, simply cut a small notch in the edge of the box opening, as shown, and slide the string into it so the fish dangles in place. Then, cover the box opening with a piece of dark-colored paper.

GLOWING FUN!

In some places, such as a small brackish (part ocean water, part fresh water) lake on the tiny Puerto Rican island of Vieques, there are so many bioluminescent fish that people actually glow when they swim there! On a moonless night, just jump in the water. The small fish react to your splashes and — abracadabra — you are glowing from head to toe.

Sea Life: Will the True Fish Please Swim By?

No doubt about it, we humans feel right at home on land. But for plenty of other species, life in the sea goes along swimmingly! Representatives from all of the major animal life forms live in the ocean. And they all have special traits that help them not only survive, but also thrive in their watery world.

Sea snakes, for instance, have bodies that are flattened side to side — just right for slicing smoothly through the water as they swim after prey. *Squid* are equipped with instant camouflage: They can squirt out ink to make the water around them very dark so they can escape from a predator in the dark of night — anytime of day! Even *krill*, shrimplike creatures that are a favorite food of whales and penguins, can jump out of their shells to confuse and (they hope!) escape a chasing predator.

You see, life in the sea is largely about eating — but not being eaten! At least nine out of ten marine creatures double as a meal for bigger and stronger animals, each one taking its place in the amazing food chain (page 34) that links all kinds of plants and animals.

But ocean life has its share of perks, too. There's plenty of room to float, swim, dive, and jump around — even if you're a whale that happens to be bigger than a jumbo jet! So, with *your* two feet planted firmly on the land, take an imaginary swim with marine life that will scare you out of your wits, make you laugh aloud at their antics, or bring a smile to your face every time you think of them.

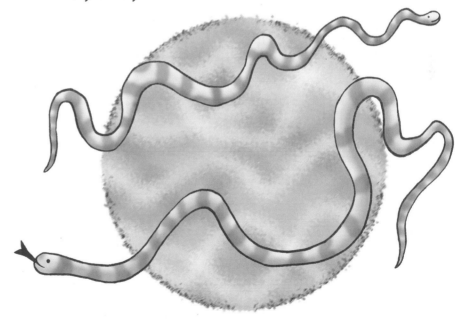

Fish Stories

Here's a snapshot of changing sea life from way back when to today ...

First came the *invertebrates*
(no backbone or spinal cord)

- Soft-bodied marine life like *jellyfish* (now known as sea jellies) and *ancient coral*
- Fish with hard plates just below their outer skin, such as *starfish* and *sea urchins*
- *Trilobites* (now extinct) were common
- Soft-bodied animals with hard shells and a powerful foot, such as *scallops* and *clams*
- Animals with segmented (divided) bodies, a hard *exoskeleton* (outside the body), and multi-jointed legs, such as crabs

Today, *9 out of every 10* animals on earth are invertebrates. Imagine that!

Then came the *vertebrates*
(animals with spinal cords or backbones)

- The most primitive fish (in the class Agnatha) were the *jawless fish*
- Next came *cartilaginous fish*, such as *sharks* and *rays*
- Then came the first "true" fish, the early *bony fish*

There you have it! Now, continue on for a closer look at some of the ocean creatures of today!

Of all the animals in the world that have a backbone (*vertebrates*), including us humans, true fish have been around the longest — for hundreds of millions of years! They also make up the largest class of vertebrates, with an estimated 30 million species or more. They belong to a major animal group — scientists call each of these groups a *phylum* — called Chordata, or chordates (same as all of us, too).

While all true fish share a few common traits with each other (backbones, fins, and gills, for starters), they vary greatly in color, shape, size, and behavior. In size alone, they range from 1" (2.5 cm) *gobies*, often seen in tide pools or swimming around the eelgrass in shallow water, to the *whale shark*, which can grow to 45' (13.5 m) long and weigh 15 tons (13.6 t). As big as it is, the whale shark was discovered less than 100 years ago! Where do you suppose it was hiding?

Shrimp!

Hey! I'm no shrimp! I'm a goby!

A PICTURE'S WORTH A THOUSAND WORDS

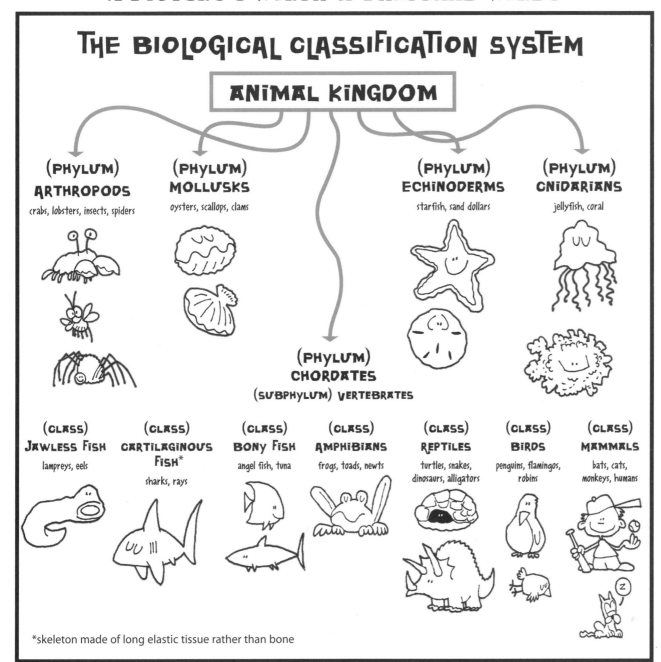

THE BIOLOGICAL CLASSIFICATION SYSTEM

ANIMAL KINGDOM

(PHYLUM) ARTHROPODS
crabs, lobsters, insects, spiders

(PHYLUM) MOLLUSKS
oysters, scallops, clams

(PHYLUM) ECHINODERMS
starfish, sand dollars

(PHYLUM) CNIDARIANS
jellyfish, coral

(PHYLUM) CHORDATES
(SUBPHYLUM) VERTEBRATES

(CLASS) JAWLESS FISH
lampreys, eels

(CLASS) CARTILAGINOUS FISH*
sharks, rays

(CLASS) BONY FISH
angel fish, tuna

(CLASS) AMPHIBIANS
frogs, toads, newts

(CLASS) REPTILES
turtles, snakes, dinosaurs, alligators

(CLASS) BIRDS
penguins, flamingos, robins

(CLASS) MAMMALS
bats, cats, monkeys, humans

*skeleton made of long elastic tissue rather than bone

CATEGORIZING TIP

In our daily lives, most of us tend to clump together all ocean sea life as "fish," but actually true fish are only one class of ocean-living animals. So if someone invites you out for a lobster dinner, better not tell your friends that you had fish last night! Uh-uh! You had an arthropod from the phylum Arthropoda (that, by the way, just happens to be the same phylum that spiders come from!). So crabs and lobsters are in the phylum Arthropoda; clams and mussels are in the phylum Mollusca; jellyfish are in the phylum Cnidaria; starfish and sand dollars are in the phylum Echinodermata; and other ocean life are in classes (now that really sounds like fish school!) in the Chordata phylum. Sharks and rays are in the "cartilaginous fish" class, lampreys and eels are in the "jawless fish" class, and the good old tuna and swordfish are in the class "bony fish," which are the only true fish. And the whale? It's in the class of mammals, just like you!

FiSH SCHooL in SeSSion

Sometimes you want to stand out in a crowd; other times it's best to blend in — like when you're a little jack fish and a great big hungry barracuda wants to swallow you whole! That's why fish of the same color, size, and shape tend to swim in *schools*. Looking and behaving just like everybody else around you makes it harder to get picked out of the crowd, but you probably know that already.

Try This! Fill a small jar with warm water and stir in a ½ teaspoon (2 ml) of single-color glitter glue until the clumps dissolve. Now focus on a single piece of glitter and see how long you can keep track of it as it swirls around. If you were a small fish, do you think you'd be safer swimming solo or in a group if a bigger predator fish decided to dine out?

In case you're wondering if fish are in school 24/7, rest assured that, like humans, fish are generally out of school at night. That's when they're off catching and eating supper. The menu? Smaller fish!

SWEEPING THROUGH

Not all predators find it hard to dine in a crowd — or is that *on* a crowd? The swordfish, with its long sharp bill, and the sawfish, equipped with a wider *serrated* (notched) snout, swim right into schools of fish, flailing their heads and slicing up a quick meal. Hungry sawfish also prowl the ocean's sandy floor for food. How do you suppose they uncover the best eating spots there?

And the sailfish wins by a sword!

FINISH

Anyone seen Flipper?

FLEET FISH

Have you ever tried running in waist-high surf? Moving quickly underwater is not all that easy. Still, fish like the sailfish and the bluefin tuna can zip right along at close to 60+ mph (97 kph) — and make it look downright easy, too! Not quite as fast but definitely respectable, the dolphin, one of our fellow mammals, clocks in at 37 mph (60 kph). Where do humans finish in this race? We're pretty much left in the wake with a top swimming speed of 5 mph (8 kph). Of course, unlike fish, we don't have the advantage of being coated with a layer of slime to help us glide smoothly through the water.

Sink & Swim

The next time you're filling the sink to wash the dinner plates, hold the soap and the dishes — to bring on the fishes! Here's a little trick that's quick to show just what it is about some fish that makes them so speedy. Then, when you're done, add suds and your supper cleanup should proceed swimmingly!

WHAT YOU NEED

- ⚓ Ruler
- ⚓ Scissors
- ⚓ 5 pieces of 18" (45 cm) string, each double-knotted at one end
- ⚓ Modeling clay
- ⚓ Sink or bathtub with a few inches (cm) of water
- ⚓ Granulated sugar

Note: Remember, even an inch (cm) or two of water is enough for a baby or toddler to drown in. Don't try this activity with a baby or toddler in the room, and always ask permission to play with water in a tub, basin, or kiddie pool — even if you are an older kid. Empty the tub when you leave the room. Thank you.

WHAT YOU DO

1. Mold a small blob of clay around one knot, making sure it's well stuck and won't fall off when you pick up the other end of the string. Roll the ball into a miniature cigar to resemble the streamlined bodies (*fusiform* shape) of fish that swim in the open ocean, like tuna, striped bass, and sharks.

2. Attach a second clay cigar to the knot on another piece of string; then pinch its sides to make a *laterally compressed* (skinny) fish, like the pumpkinseeds, butterfly fish, and triggerfish that school in shallow water and maneuver around coral reefs.

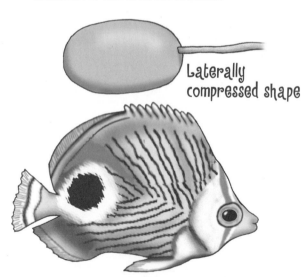

Laterally compressed shape

Four-Eyed Butterfly Fish

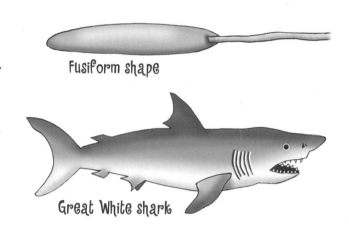

Fusiform shape

Great White shark

3. For your third fish, hold a clay cigar horizontally and pull the cigar slightly from the top and bottom to shape a flat ray, skate, or other bottom-dweller with a *depressed* body shape.

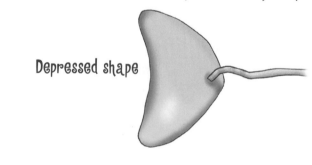

Depressed shape

Skate ray

4. Finally, mold a *round* puffer and also a *cube-shaped* boxfish from clay, both types of fish that usually are equipped with a powerful *toxin* (poison) to fend off predators they can't outswim. Attach a length of string to each one.

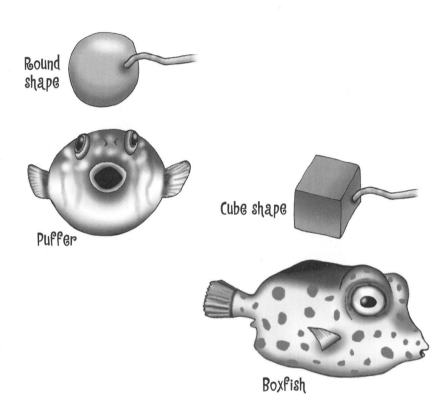

Round shape

Puffer

Cube shape

Boxfish

5. One at a time, tow your fish through the water. Which is easiest to pull, offering the least resistance? Moves the straightest? Creates the greatest wake (turbulence), and therefore resistance? If you were a fish trying to get away, which shape would you want to be?

What's Happening?

Fish with fusiform body shapes move the quickest and most smoothly through the water, particularly in the open ocean away from coral reefs and areas where seaweed grows. Laterally compressed fish don't swim as fast as fusiform fish, but their body shape allows them to slide efficiently around and between underwater plants. Fish with depressed bodies are slow swimmers, but they are designed to burrow into the sand to hide from predators. Round and cube-shaped fish are pretty slow, too, but generally are equipped with spines or poisons to protect themselves.

CUBIC CRUISER

With scales that are fused together, cube-shaped boxfish can't propel themselves along by bending their bodies in S-shaped curves the way most fish can. Instead, they use their *pectoral* (side) fins to paddle along — a trait that also lets them spin their 2" (5 cm) square bodies around in any direction! That's why U.S. Navy researchers have kept a watchful eye on three of these bright yellow, black-spotted reef fish that they named King Kong, Nessie, and Jaws. The hope is that engineers will be able to mimic the boxfish's maneuverability to build a brand-new research-and-rescue submarine that can turn on a dime, even in the strong underwater currents along the ocean floor. Give your clay boxfish a whirl underwater to see how it spins.

Unsinkable Fish

Just like us, most marine animals have flesh and bones that make them heavier than water. That's why many fast open-ocean swimmers, like tuna and squid, will start to slowly sink as soon as they stop swimming. But some rock and reef fish are equipped with a special gas-filled chamber called a swim bladder *(sort of like a built-in life preserver) that allows them to rise, descend, or stay put at different water levels. By increasing the amount of gas, they can make themselves bigger without increasing their weight to make themselves more* buoyant *(float more easily).*

Sharks don't have a swim bladder to boost their buoyancy, so they have to get a little lift from their large oil-filled livers.

WHAT YOU NEED

- ⚓ 3 small balloons (different colors)
- ⚓ Water
- ⚓ Vegetable oil
- ⚓ Funnel
- ⚓ 3 rubber bands
- ⚓ 3 pennies
- ⚓ Sink or large glass bowl filled with water

WHAT YOU DO

1. Fill one balloon with air (for a fish with a swim bladder); one with water (for an animal without a swim bladder); and one with oil (for a shark with an oil-filled liver).

Note: It's easier to fill balloons if you stretch the neck over the tip of a funnel — fill them just enough to give them shape.

2. Tightly wind a rubber band around the neck of each balloon. Then insert a penny for weight into the end of each balloon neck (the fish's "tail").

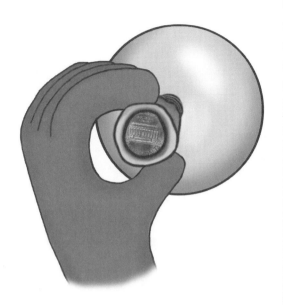

3. Place the balloons in the water-filled sink and watch what happens! Which animal do you think has the advantage when it comes to staying afloat?

BUBBLING SEAWEED

Fish breathe by gulping in seawater and passing it over their *gills*, where oxygen is absorbed right out of the water into their blood. Gills are thin flaps of tissue — think of the underside of a mushroom. Lucky for the fish: Not only do waves, wind, and rain churn oxygen into the seas, but seaweed, algae, and other marine plants actually make it. In fact, these plants produce more oxygen than all the *terrestrial* (land) plants put together!

I can blow bubbles, too!

Try This! Ask an adult if you can have a few clippings from a houseplant or an outdoor shrub. Fill a medium-sized mixing bowl halfway with water. Then, put the clippings in a clean glass jar and fill the jar to the rim with water. Holding a square of cardboard tightly against the rim, turn the jar over and set it down in the bowl (you can remove the cardboard once the rim is under water). Leave the bowl in a sunny place for an hour or two. Then, check out the leaves. Notice anything?

What's Happening?

Plants use sunlight, carbon dioxide, and water to make food (it's that process of photosynthesis again), and in the process they release oxygen through their leaves. That's why the leaves in your jar are covered with tiny bubbles.

PLease DON'T WRITe in

WHAT'S IN A NAME?

Well, sometimes enough to get an idea of what a fish looks like. See if you can match up the following fish descriptions with the proper names. Grab a piece of scrap paper, and copy the numbered names in a vertical column near the paper's left margin. Then print the letter of the answer you think best describes each fish next to its name. To see how you did, check out the answer key at the bottom of the next page.

1. barber fish

2. wolf eel

3. mudskippers

4. stonefish

5. sarcastic fringeheads

6. lionfish

7. stargazer

8. porcupine fish

9. parrot fish

10. hatchet fish

11. four-eyed butterfly fish

A. During low tide, these fish use their armlike appendages to hop around shores where mangrove trees grow.

B. These fish may look like they're grinning, but they have a reputation for being pretty ill-tempered. When two of them duke it out for territory, the one with the biggest mouth wins.

C. These silvery deep-sea fish have blade-shaped bodies.

D. A pair of big black spots near this fish's tail can fool a predator into thinking the fish is coming when it's really going.

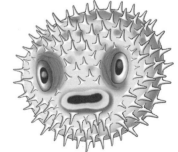

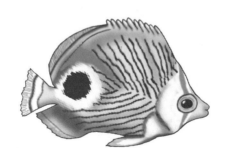

THiS BOOK. THank You.

E. This resident of the Indian and Pacific oceans has a "mane" made of hollow, poisonous spines.

F. You won't catch this fish shying away from sharks; in fact, grooming sharks is its favorite pasttime.

G. This fish has a beaklike mouth equipped for crunching and munching coral.

H. This fierce-looking fish has sharp teeth, but it's very friendly and can easily be lured out of its rocky den to eat food (like sea urchins) out of a diver's hands.

I. When frightened, this spine-covered fish blows up like a beach ball to make itself hard for predators to swallow.

J. It looks as harmless as a weed-covered rock, but this fish uses its spine to stick its enemy with deadly venom.

K. This unusual-looking creature points its eyes directly upward and waits for prey to swim overhead.

Now see if you can find each fish's image floating around these pages.

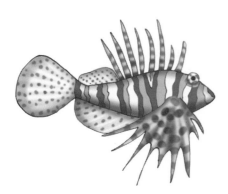

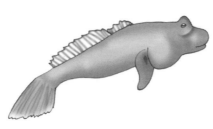

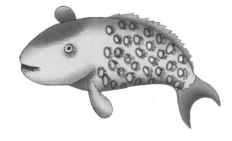

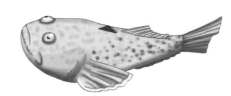

What's in a Name?

Answers: 1.F; 2,H; 3, A; 4, J; 5, B; 6, E; 7, K; 8, I; 9, G; 10, C; 11, D

79

Missing:
A Backbone

When it comes to being a fish, it takes more than a home in the ocean or even a name to make the claim, as you know. No matter what we call them, without backbones, they're *invertebrates* — so they just don't qualify as true fish! Take a look back at the animal kingdom chart on page 71. You'll find lots of nonfish sea life there.

THE ANIMAL FORMERLY KNOWN AS JELLYFISH

One invertebrate in the phylum Cnidaria, the jellyfish, now newly named the *sea jelly*, is missing more than a backbone — it doesn't have a heart, a brain, or gills either! (It *really* needs a trip to Oz with Dorothy!) It does, however, have muscles strong enough to squeeze together its hollow bell-shaped body and push out water to propel itself along. And, as harmless as it may look, a sea jelly can be quite the predator! Its long trailing tentacles, which "net" all kinds of small animal organisms to eat — including fish eggs and other sea jellies — are covered with stinging cells. Each one of these cells can shoot a tiny *harpoon* (little needle with a venom sac attached) filled with a *toxin* (poison) that can stun or even kill its prey — even after the sea jelly itself has died! (So don't touch a dead one on the beach!)

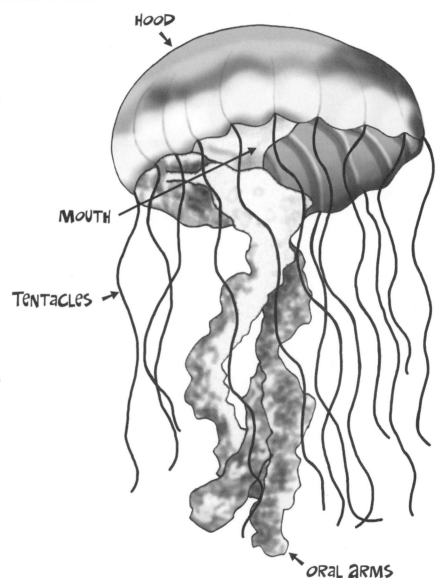

HOOD

MOUTH

TENTACLES →

ORAL ARMS

Race a Squid

Like its cousin the octopus, a squid has eight sucker-covered arms plus two tentacles to capture fish and crabs as it moves in zigzag fashion through the water. Its powerful muscles contract to force out jets of water that propel it in the opposite direction — so it swims backward — and oh, so fast! Plus, it can shoot out an inky fluid and then quickly dart into the middle of it to hide from a pursuer! Considered a delicacy, the squid has become endangered in some parts of the world.

Try This! Fill the bathtub or a sink with water. Then, fill a balloon with water and, while you keep the neck pinched closed, have a friend stretch the lip up over a closed squirt cap (the type that comes on a sports-drink bottle works particularly well). Hold your balloon "squid" underwater at one end of the tub or sink, open the cap nozzle, and let go. Water will shoot out of the bottle and propel the balloon in the opposite direction — just like a real squid.

Note: Remember, even an inch (cm) or two of water is enough for a baby or toddler to drown in. Don't try this activity with a baby or toddler in the room, and always ask permission to play with water in a tub, basin, or kiddie pool — even if you are an older kid. Empty the tub when you leave the room. Thank you.

Ocean Gazette

July 27, 2002:
Giant Squid Pile Up on California Beach

Twelve tons (11 t) of giant squid tumbled in with the surf and were stranded on San Diego's (U.S.) La Jolla Cove beach today after chasing a school of grunion, a fish that lays its eggs on the sand at high tide. The squid generally don't show up this far north, but scientists suspect they've caught a ride with El Niño's warm-water currents (page 35).

SNAPPY SHRIMP

What do crickets and shrimp have in common? Besides being arthropods (page 71), they both can make a big racket! Chances are you've heard the loud chirp of a cricket on a summer night, but what about the sharp click of a little shrimp snapping shut its claw? This lightning-quick motion sends out a shock wave strong enough to stun a worm or other potential meal! In big schools of shrimp, the snapping sounds like the crackle of french fries cooking in hot oil. Sometimes it's loud enough to drown out submarine communications! To hear the crackle and pop of snapping shrimp (and a host of other sea creature sounds), log on to **<http://oceanlink.island.net/oinfo/acoustics/ListenLinks.html>**.

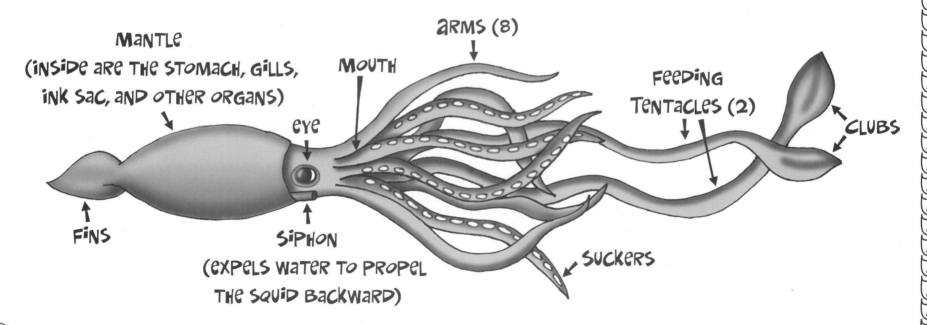

MANTLE
(INSIDE ARE THE STOMACH, GILLS, INK SAC, AND OTHER ORGANS)

MOUTH

ARMS (8)

FEEDING TENTACLES (2)

CLUBS

EYE

FINS

SIPHON
(EXPELS WATER TO PROPEL THE SQUID BACKWARD)

SUCKERS

Marine Mammals

Animals had lived in the ocean for a long time — billions of years, in fact! — before any of them ended up on land. And when they finally did, it was more a matter of chance than anything. As more and more life filled the ocean, all kinds of plants and fishlike animals began washing ashore with the tides. In time, some of those animals grew limbs and crawled farther inland. From them, new species of land reptiles, and then mammals, evolved. But then, about 5 to 10 million years ago, the world's climate cooled, and some of those mammals began hunting offshore where food was more plentiful. Eventually, they wound up living in the water full-time.

Today, marine mammals, such as whales, dolphins, and seals, still share some of the same traits as their cousins on land — like breathing through lungs (instead of gills) and giving birth to live young. But they've also made some amazing adaptations. In most cases, their limbs have evolved into flippers and they've packed on an extra-thick layer of fat to help stay warm, making them well equipped to inhabit even the coldest oceans.

Go on a Whale Walk

Every year crowds of tourists board whale-watching boats and head out to sea where they hope to catch sight of one of these aquatic giants. It may be hard to believe, but 50 million years ago, whale-watchers would have had to ride around on buses instead — if buses had been invented, that is! That's when the whale's earliest known ancestor, a furry, four-legged meat-eater named *Pakicetus*, lived on land. Within a mere 10 million years (scientists say that's not very long in the grand evolutionary scheme), this landlubber became a seafarer.

Today, the blue whale, weighing up to 160 tons (145 t), is the biggest animal living — or to have ever lived — on earth! By the time it's just 1 or 2 weeks old, it's as big as an elephant; full grown, it can weigh as much as 25 elephants. And, reaching lengths greater than 100' (30 m), it can be longer than a basketball court. The reason whales can get so big is that the water in the ocean helps hold up their incredible tonnage. But when a whale gets stranded on a beach, its own weight can crush its internal organs.

Whale Tales

Of all the mammals living in the sea, the whale is probably the most at home there. The *sperm whale*, just one of the 78 whale species scientists have identified so far, can dive deeper and stay underwater longer than any other mammal (like all mammals, though, it eventually must surface to take a breath). The *gray whale* is the long-distance champ, swimming as many as 12,500 miles (20,113 km) every spring as it migrates from its breeding grounds in the warm waters off Mexico all the way to its summer feeding grounds in the Arctic. And with plenty of room to grow, the *blue whale* just keeps on growing older and older (and bigger, too) until it's nearly 30 years old!

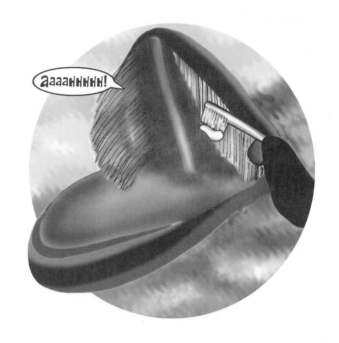

aaaaнннны!

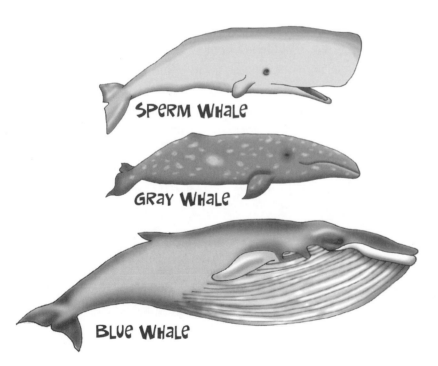

SPERM WHALE

GRAY WHALE

BLUE WHALE

A Whale of an Appetite

Most whales — including dolphins, which make up the largest family of whales, and porpoises — have plenty of teeth for hunting fish and squid. But, with the exception of sperm whales (like Moby Dick), all of the biggest whales are toothless! Instead, their mouths are filled with tough and springy comblike strainers called baleen *that hang down like rows of curtains. When a baleen whale wants to feed, it swims along with its jaws wide open and gulps in water filled with plankton. Then, it uses its tongue to squeeze the water out the sides of its mouth and lick back the plankton sifted out by its baleen. Even though plankton can be as tiny as a grain of rice, this efficient filtering system can easily collect enough of them to satisfy even a whale of an appetite!*

WHAT YOU NEED

- ⚓ Clean plastic gallon (3.7 L) jug (the kind milk and juice come in)
- ⚓ Permanent colored marker
- ⚓ Craft knife
- ⚓ Large baking pan
- ⚓ Water
- ⚓ Teaspoon
- ⚓ Dried herbs, such as oregano or parsley, or glitter

WHAT YOU DO

1. Holding the jug on its side with the handle at the top so it resembles a whale's head, outline a whale's mouth and eye as shown.

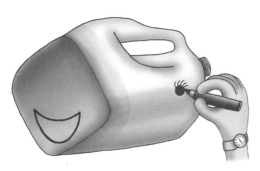

Note: A real whale has baleen on both sides, but for this activity, one side will do fine.

2. Ask an adult to help cut out the mouth. To simulate a whale's baleen, outline the shape and a series of vertical lines along one side of the "jaw." Cut along the lines to form slits.

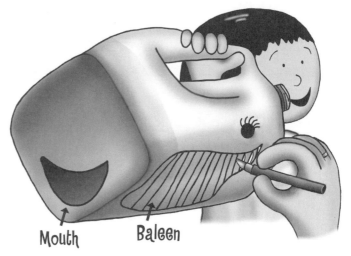

Mouth   Baleen

3. Fill the baking pan halfway with water. Stir in a couple of teaspoons (10 ml) of dried herbs or glitter for *krill* (the small shrimplike plankton), and you're ready to fish for lunch, whale-style. Grasp the jug by the handle, and with the baleen facing the bottom of the pan, slowly scoop water into the mouth of the whale (just as a gray whale rolls on its side to suck food-filled mud from the ocean floor). Now lift the jug just above the pan so the water can drain through the baleen. How successful was your quest for lunch?

"Seal" in the Warmth

Diving into the icy cold water around the North and South poles is enough to make you "blubber" — unless you happen to have a layer of blubber (extra thick body fat), like seals, whales, and other animals that live there. Not only is blubber a good insulator (a substance that keeps warmth from escaping), it also helps block out excess heat from the sun so a seal can catch a snooze on the ice before it has to dive back in the water to cool off.

WHAT YOU NEED

⚓ Bowl
⚓ Water
⚓ Ice cubes
⚓ Spoon
⚓ Solid vegetable shortening (like Crisco)
⚓ 2 plastic bags
⚓ Large rubber band

WHAT YOU DO

1. Fill the bowl three-fourths of the way with the water and ice cubes. This will serve as your mini Arctic Ocean.

2. Spoon two or three large scoops of the vegetable shortening into the bottom of one plastic bag. Slip your hand into the other bag, and then insert it into the "shortening" bag. (Don't worry, your skin never directly touches the fat!) Use the rubber band to secure the two bags around your wrist. Use your free hand to squeeze the outer bag, packing the shortening all around your fingers.

3. Now you're ready to take the big plunge: Submerge your fingers right into the ice water. Are you surprised by what happens? See how all that blubber works for a whale?

Mmm... nice and toasty!

What's Happening?

Your hand stays toasty warm because, like blubber, the shortening packed around it prevents body heat from escaping, and at the same time, seals out the cold of the ice water.

Q: Are humans warm-blooded or cold-blooded?

A: What's your temperature in a warm bathtub and out in the snow? Some answer, eh? But that answer really is the answer. Now we're not talking about when you have a fever; we're talking about your body temperature, which is usually around 98.6°F (37°C).

If your body temperature is about the same when you are in a hot bathtub and when you are in the snow (or in a cold shower), then you are *warm-blooded*. That means that you, and all of us mammals, have about the same body temperature no matter what environment you are in (unless you are ill).

Now a fish, on the other hand, changes body temperature: If it's in warm water, its temperature will rise and if it is in cold water, its temperature will fall. So a fish is *cold-blooded*.

Lunching Like an Otter

Unlike seals and other ocean mammals that have blubber, a sea otter relies on its dense double layer of fur and food — lots of food! — to keep warm. To generate enough body heat to survive in the cold ocean waters, these critters need to consume 30 percent of their own weight in food every day! For an average 90-pound (40.5-kg) otter, that's about 27 pounds (13.5 kg) of shellfish each day. Floating on its back, it uses its belly as a tabletop on which it breaks open clams with a stone. And every so often, it rolls in the water to wash off the dinner table!

Just like humans, individual otters have their favorite foods. So, sometimes the menu includes sea cucumbers, octopuses, and sea urchins. Imagine if you had to eat as much as an otter to keep toasty. How many $\frac{1}{4}$- pound (125-g) burgers or 18-ounce (450-g) jars of peanut butter would it take?

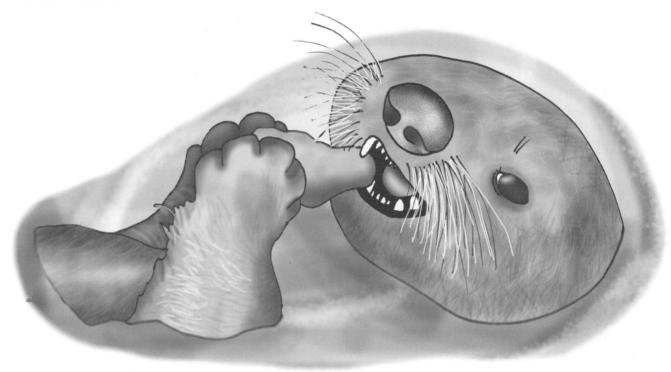

THOSE MYTHICAL MAIDENS OF THE SEA

Believe it or not, the mermaid would more aptly have been named a moo-maid. Blame it on the fog or a bad case of seasickness, but the beautiful half woman/half fish creatures early sailors claimed to have seen were probably sea cows, or manatees! That's right! These 6' to 10' (1.8 to 3 m) sea mammals are known to stand up on their tails and hold their calves in their arms, a trait that could make them look humanlike from a distance — a *long* distance. With bald heads, whiskered faces, and a habit of chomping their teeth and flapping their lips when they eat, sea cows aren't exactly ladylike, but they sure must have fooled some sailors!

Still, the sea cow's friendliness toward man makes it a most endearing creature of the sea, so our affection for them is certainly not misplaced. Too much so for the sea cow's own good, perhaps. The 30' (9 m) *Steller's sea cow*, the largest species in the group, became extinct at the beginning of the 19th century when Bering Sea whalers hunted it continually. There are just two species alive today. The manatee occupies tropical estuaries along the gulf coast of Florida, in the Caribbean, and along Central America and West Africa where it keeps the waterways clear of water hyacinth, a plant it loves to eat. Its cousin, the *dugong*, lives along the coasts of the Indian Ocean, the Red Sea, and the western Pacific, grazing on eelgrass and waterweeds.

ADOPT A MANATEE

If you want to learn more about manatees, consider adopting one through the Save the Manatee Club's Adopt-A-Manatee program. This nonprofit organization works to protect, rescue, and advocate for these gentle sea creatures. The club keeps close tabs on more than two dozen adoptees residing in Florida's Blue Spring and Homosassa Springs Wildlife state parks, and in Tampa Bay. You can read about all the potential adoptees — like Philip, who's known for following the research canoe, and Lorelei, who likes to do barrel rolls when she swims — and get regular updates on how they're doing at <www.savethemanatee.org/adoptpag.htm>.

Don't hate me because I'm beautiful!

Sea Birds

When most birds head south for the winter to escape the cold, *Adélie penguins* make the frostiest, windiest place in the world their year-round home. And that place just so happens to be as far south as you can get — at the South Pole. All 17 penguin species live south of the equator, where they dive for fish. To recognize fellow members of their own group, penguins look for the distinctive markings of their species.

WHAT YOU NEED

⚓ Glue stick
⚓ Craft foam, one 2" (5 cm) black square and one 2" (5 cm) white square
⚓ Scissors
⚓ Glass jar
⚓ Water
⚓ Black paper

WHAT YOU DO

1. Glue the two craft-foam squares together, one on top of the other. Then, cut out a simple penguin shape (or any other shape you choose).

The Well-Dressed Penguin

Just because you're a bird doesn't mean you can fly. Take the penguin: With solid, heavy bones (unlike the hollow, light ones most birds have) and wings that are more like paddles, the penguin is better equipped to swim. (Not to mention it's got a great bathing suit!) It's stylish tuxedo can disappear in the flash of a predator's eye, thanks to a mode of disguise called countershading. *From above, the penguin's black back blends into the dark of the ocean depths, while from below, its white belly fades into the light at the water's surface. But don't take our word for it — see how countershading works for yourself!*

2. Fill the jar halfway with water and float the penguin with the black side down on top of the water. Hold the jar up under an overhead light and look at the penguin through the bottom of the jar. It should be clearly visible.

3. Now, flip the penguin over so the white side is down (the way a penguin swims), and look again. Its shape isn't nearly as noticeable! Its white belly blends in with the light surface of the water, making it harder for predators to spot the bird from below — just like a real penguin in the ocean.

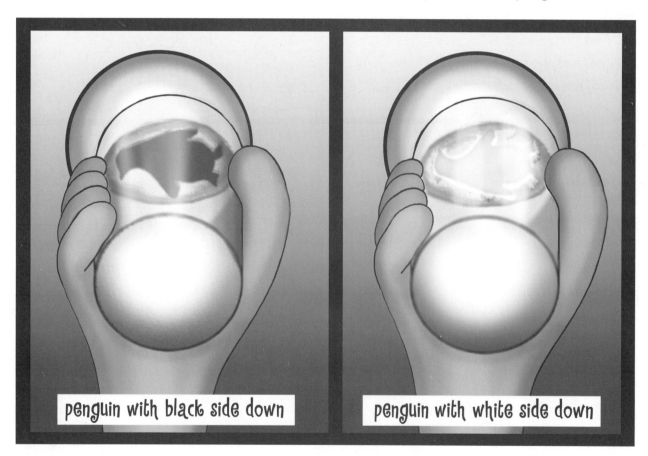

penguin with black side down

penguin with white side down

4. Set the jar down on the black paper (the paper resembles how dark it is in the ocean). Take a look (from overhead this time) to see how the black side of the penguin's tux also helps it blend into the water. See how nature works to protect these special creatures?

Seafaring Reptiles

Early sailors were probably the first people to lay eyes on many of the marine animals that are so familiar to us today. Oftentimes, as tales of those encounters were relayed from port to port, descriptions of those "unusual" creatures got grander and scarier based purely on speculations of what that creature might be able to do! Sometimes stories even circulated about animals that *might* exist. The Vikings (early sea explorers from northern Europe), for example, told of a giant wriggling serpent that started ocean storms. Greek legends mentioned a serpent, too — one with many heads!

The truth is that more than 50 species of snakes, most of which are poisonous, do live in the ocean — generally in the seas around Australia, Indonesia, Southeast Asia, and India. None have any noticeable effect on the weather, though. And they come with just one head per body. That's

not to say they're without some interesting features, such as tails that are shaped like rudders for steering their bodies through the water. Plus, with lungs that are nearly as long as their bodies and nostrils with closable flaps, these snakes are well equipped to stay underwater for hours!

TURTLE TEARS

Ocean creatures whose ancestors once lived on land like the sea turtle have body fluids that aren't nearly as salty as the seawater they swim in. Since salt draws moisture from its environment, these animals can *dehydrate* (lose too much water from their bodies). It's enough to make a turtle cry. Really! To maintain the right *salinity* (level of salt), sea turtles have big tear glands that condense excess salt and squeeze it out in huge, salty tears!

TRYING TIMES FOR TURTLES

To watch a sea turtle gracefully glide through the water, sometimes as speedily as 35 mph (56 kph), you'd never suspect it was related to a certain lumbering land tortoise whose only racing victory was beating an opponent who fell asleep on the way to the finish line. Using their front flippers as paddles and their back ones to steer, sea turtles make great time as they migrate amazing distances. The *Pacific loggerhead sea turtle*, for example, swims some 7,500 miles (12,067 km) between its nesting beach in Japan to its favorite feeding grounds near Baja, California. How's that for going out to dinner?

Even though sea turtles have been cruising the seas for millions of years, today all seven species (the *Australian flatback*, *green*, *hawksbill*, *Kemp's ridley*, *leatherback*, *loggerhead*, and *olive ridley*) are endangered or threatened species. (Could you imagine a world without turtles?) One of the biggest problems facing them is pollution. Many a plastic bag has turned into a deadly meal for a hungry turtle who thought it was swallowing a jellyfish. And, until recently, tens of thousands of sea turtles were snagged and drowned every year in the drag nets used to catch shrimp.

Thankfully, all U.S. shrimpers now must install **T**urtle **E**xcluder **D**evices (TEDs) in their nets. A TED looks like a round grate (the kind in a barbecue grill) with bars that are too close together for a turtle to get through. It fits snugly down into the narrow neck of the net, and right beside it is an opening. When a turtle that's been scooped into the drag net comes to the grate, it can swim straight out the opening. (Shrimp, on the other hand, keep right on going through the grate and into the bottom of the net.) Visit **<http://library.thinkquest.org/11137/teds.html>** to watch a short video about how a TED works.

I love TEDs!

Caution: Baby Turtle Crossing

Growing up to be an adult sea turtle is no simple feat. For starters, babies have to hatch themselves since their moms always head straight back into the surf after laying their eggs in pits above the high-tide mark. Once they've broken through their shells, it can take a nestful of hatchlings several days to dig their way up through the sand. Then, under the cover of darkness when hungry birds or crabs are less likely to spot them, the hatchlings make their break for the sea with only the shimmering moonlight to guide them.

Orienting themselves toward the brightest horizon is an instinct that's always served them well — until recently. As more building goes on in coastal areas, artificial lighting from houses and businesses draws many a turtle way off course. Crawling on the beach for hours, especially in the wrong direction, can leave these little lost souls too exhausted to ever make it to the ocean.

For those hatchlings that do manage to get their feet wet, the next task is to swim several miles (km) offshore to be swept up in currents filled with nourishing seaweed — a floating turtle nursery of sorts. Even then, with the threat of being swallowed up by hungry sharks and other big fish, *only about one in a thousand hatchlings will make it to adulthood!* That sure is slim pickings compared with other animal hatchlings, like the desert tortoise which has a survival rate of 1 to 5 per 100 and the alligator with a survival rate of 1 in 10.

Try This! Set a large bowl of water on a table in front of a wall and jiggle it slightly to start some mini waves. Standing in front of the bowl, shine a flashlight at a 45° angle onto the water surface. You should see a dancing pattern of light appear on the wall behind the bowl — the very type of reflection that guides turtle hatchlings to the sea.

Saving Our Seas: Stand Up & Be Counted!

Since ancient times, when the first fishermen crafted wooden spears tipped with stone points, man has turned to the ocean for food. Today, with more than half the world's people undernourished, we're counting more than ever on the "sea of plenty" to continue to provide. Food isn't the only resource that world leaders are looking to the ocean for. Thousands of *desalination* plants are separating salt from seawater to create more fresh drinking water. Reserves of oil and gas under the seafloor are being tapped to help alleviate the crunch on other fuel supplies, too. Yes, the ocean could play a major role in saving the people on earth — that is, if the people on earth work together to save the ocean!

Fishing Versus Overfishing

More than 500 years ago, John Cabot, a European explorer, discovered one of the richest fishing grounds the world has ever known. Off the coast of present-day Newfoundland (eastern Canada), the water was so thick with codfish it was said you could scoop them up in a basket! Thanks to the shallower waters of this area, called the Grand Banks, and the warm Gulf Stream current that flows through them, crabs and shrimp also hung out there, providing perfect feeding grounds for cod and other fish. It was nature working in perfect balance!

And, indeed, codfish were easily scooped from the Grand Banks (a *bank* is a slightly elevated undersea area). Fishery scientists estimate that some

8 million tons (7.3 million t) of northern cod were harvested in the 300 years following Cabot's discovery! If that sounds like a lot, think about this: Today's fleet of industrial fishing boats has caught the same amount in *only 15 years!* Using nets as big as several football fields linked together, these "factory trawlers" can trap up to 400 tons (363 t) in one haul!

If you are thinking, "Great! Codfish for all!" think again. Since a codfish lives about 20 years, an entire generation can be wiped out before the next one is in place. Uh-oh. You know what that could mean — eventual *extinction* (permanent elimination)!

Aw, Mom! Do we have to have codfish again for dinner?

Heavy Concepts

If you're having difficulty imagining how much a ton weighs (not to mention 400 tons), here's some help:

How much one codfish weighs: **20 to 25 pounds (9 to 11 kg)** — **the weight of an average watermelon!**

Weighing in at about one ton (.9 t): **A regular-sized pickup truck (1 ton = 2,000 pounds or .907 metric ton)**

Weighing in at about 400 tons (363 t): **A jumbo jet!**

Setting Limits

Every year, 75 million tons (68 million t) or more of fish are hauled from the ocean. Is that too many? Well, the answer seems to vary depending upon whom you ask. The key is striking the right balance between what we take and the number left behind to reproduce so the size of the fish population is maintained. But that is not a simple thing to agree on. One way governments try to prevent overfishing is to put a limit, or *quota*, on the yearly catches.

In 1988, when fishery scientists realized how depleted the codfish population was along Canada's Grand Banks, they recommended lowering the quota by at least 50 percent (so for every 100 fish they used to catch, now they could only catch 50). But politicians were worried more about how smaller catches would hurt the economy, and so their compromise was to lower the quota by only 10 percent (for every 100 fish they used to catch, now they can catch 90). Just four years later, so few codfish were left, fishermen were catching only a fraction of the allowable quota anyway! By then, it was too late. The Canadian government had to close the famous Grand Banks fishing grounds to give the codfish a chance to recover — but it's possible they never will.

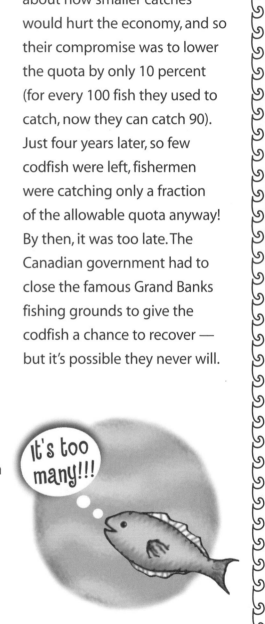

It's too many!!!

Focus on the Issues

How many fish should the fishermen catch?

Scientists: Catch only as many as will allow maintenance of fish population.

Small-fleet fishermen: Catch as many as you can, so all fishermen will be able to earn a living and keep their jobs.

Large "factory trawler" fishermen: Catch as many as you can sell, so fishermen will be employed and people will have a healthy, inexpensive food source.

Government: Catch as many as are necessary to keep the fishing economy healthy and the environment healthy, too.

Fish: Leave adequate amounts of fish so we can reproduce enough to continue our existence and keep the food chain unbroken.

What Would You Do?

Suppose the decision was yours to make, Ambassador of the Ocean. On one hand you have people who depend on catching fish to earn a living. When Canada banned fishing for cod off Newfoundland, families that had worked at sea for many generations suddenly couldn't catch enough fish to earn enough money to pay their bills. Fifty thousand fishermen and factory workers lost their jobs! On the other hand, if the predictions by fishery scientists are accurate, and no limits are set, you run the risk of wiping out an entire species! Can you think of any way to protect the fish without causing a financial burden for the fishermen and fishing industry?

Estimating Fish Populations

To come up with logical quotas that will help prevent species from being depleted in a certain area, first you need to know how many fish live there now. Of course, counting them one at a time isn't possible. Here's what scientists do:

(1) *Catch and tag some of the fish in a specific location, and then release them.*

(2) *Periodically return to the same location and catch additional batches.*

(3) *Tally the total number of fish caught in each batch as well as the number of tagged fish caught.*

Using those totals, scientists can work up some fairly accurate estimates of the total population. So, be a scientist and see how this works.

What You Need

- Large plastic yogurt (or similar) container with a cover
- Ruler
- Craft knife
- Box of toothpicks
- Colored marker
- Paper and pencil
- Calculator

What You Do

1. Ask an adult to help you cut a slot in the container cover (about 1/4" x 2", or 5 mm x 5 cm). Without counting them, dump all of the toothpicks ("fish") into the container ("ocean") and put on the cover.

2. Hold the container upside down a few inches (cm) above a tabletop and give it five good shakes so that some of the toothpicks ("fish") fall out. Write down the number in that batch (let's suppose you got 22). Tag each one with a colored mark and return all of the colored (tagged) "fish" to the container.

3. Cap the container and, holding your hand over the opening, shake it vigorously to mix up all the fish. Now it's time to see what will come up in your next catch. Repeat the shaking part of step 2 (let's say you got 20 toothpick "fish" this time). Now count up how many of them are tagged (suppose there are 4).

Catch, then tag first batch

Tally tagged and total fish per catch

To find out how many similar batches it would take to recover all of the *tagged* fish, divide the number of fish you tagged in your first batch (22) by the number of tagged fish you "caught" in the next batch (4). Your answer (5.5) multiplied by the number of fish you caught in step 3 (20) equals an estimated total of *all the fish* in the area (110).

4. Starting again with *all* of the tagged and untagged fish placed back into the container, repeat step 3 four more times. Record your results. Then add up the five estimated totals (be sure to use your results — not my examples shown below) and divide by 5 to get the average. Once you have your final estimate of the number of fish in the area, count all of the toothpicks and see how close you are to the real total.

PUTTING THE NUMBERS TO WORK! Once the number of fish is determined, scientists use that information and other important factors — such as the species' life span and the effects of changes in the environment — to set reasonable fishing limits. The key is to make sure that with all the fish caught by fishermen plus those lost to pollution and other causes, there will still be enough left in the ocean to mature and reproduce at a rate that keeps the population from getting smaller.

TAGGED FISH = 22

Total Fish in Catch/ Tagged Fish in Catch	Total Tagged Fish ÷ Tagged Fish in Catch = Number of Catches to Recover All Tagged Fish	Number of Catches x Total Fish in that Catch = Estimate of Total Fish in Area	Total Fish in 5 Catches ÷ 5 (# of times you fished) = Average Estimate of Total Population
20 / 4	22 ÷ 4 = 5.5	5.5 x 20 = 110	509 ÷ 5 = 101.8 or 102 fish
9 / 2	22 ÷ 2 = 11	11 x 9 = 99	
30 / 7	22 ÷ 7 = 3.1	3.1 x 30 = 93	
25 / 5	22 ÷ 5 = 4.4	4.4 x 25 = 110	
22 / 5	22 ÷ 5 = 4.4	4.4 x 22 = 96.8	

BREAKING THE FOOD CHAIN

And there is one more major concern about overfishing — the food chain! The *food chain* is just that — a series of plants and animals linked together because each kind is a source of food for the next one on the chain. Every time one *species* (type) is threatened, all the others linked to it are affected, too. Codfish isn't the only species whose numbers are at an all-time low. Peruvian and South African anchovy, Alaskan pollock and king crab, and California sardine populations are declining, too. If the numbers continue to dwindle, it'll mean a lot more than a smaller selection of fish at the market.

During the last 30 years while commercial fishing boats have hauled more and more pollock from the northern Pacific, the Alaskan population of Steller sea lions, which feeds on pollock, has fallen to a mere fifth of what it used to be! What do you think that eventually might mean for sea lion predators, such as the killer whale and white shark, as well as for the species that are linked to the other end of the chain, like the zooplankton (page 34) that pollock feed on? And because pollock and herring often compete for zooplankton, how do you think the balance between these three species will be affected?

Try This! Print the names *zooplankton, pollock, sea lions,* and *killer whales* on separate slips of paper and arrange them in the order in which the animals feed. Now remove one of the animals from the middle of your food chain and think about what effect its disappearance is likely to have on the species that feed on it. And that's just the half of it. Consider what will happen to the population of the species that's normally eaten by the animal you took away — and so on. Rather complicated — and scary!

Awesome Ocean Science!

Needed:
Pollution Patrols

Coral colonies sometimes look like branching trees, tiny individual flowers, fans, organ pipes, large domes — even miniature brains (called *brain coral*, of course). In fact, some coral look so much like plants that many people think live coral *are* plants! But as you know from the chart of the animal kingdom (page 71), coral *polyps* (as these itty-bitty creatures are called) are animals — some of the most beautiful animals of the ocean.

Coral polyps live in large clusters called colonies, and each animal filters a mineral called *calcium carbonate* (limestone) right out of the water. It uses this mineral to make a solid skeleton around itself to live in that looks like a hard, stony "cup" about the size of a baby's fingernail. As old polyps die off, others build a new layer right on top of these skeletons, forming elaborate *reefs* (underwater ridges of rock, sand, or, in this case, coral). Many of these reefs have been growing for thousands, even millions, of years and include *billions* of cups. The Great Barrier Reef off the coast of Australia is so big — about 1,250 miles (2,011 km) long — that it shows up in pictures taken from outer space! (For an interesting read, try *A Walk on the Great Barrier Reef* by Caroline Arnold to learn more about this amazing coral reef and the fish that live there.)

Unfortunately, these age-old coral reefs are in danger of being destroyed by harvesting for coral jewelry, by scuba divers accidentally touching and breaking off the fragile coral, and … by pollution.

Carnation Coral

Pillar Coral

Sea Fan & Brain Coral

Elkhorn Coral

101

Here's the problem: The tiny coral polyps depend on algae for food. And algae only grow where the water is clear and shallow enough for sunlight to pass through, keeping the temperature above 68°F (20°C). You see algae, like all plants, have the amazing ability to make their own food with only one key ingredient: sunlight. Sunlight usually passes through the shallower water over a reef without a problem. But pollutants or soils that end up in the ocean can block the rays from filtering through. See for yourself:

Try This! Fill two drinking glasses with water and stir ½ teaspoon (2 ml) of flour (the pollutant) into one of them. Set the glasses on a sunny windowsill or in front of a light. See how light passes right through the plain water? What happens to the rays trying to pass through the other glass? There you have it: Pollution blocks sun, algae can't survive, and the coral dies off.

Awesome Ocean Science!

CORAL CITY

With lots of nooks and crannies to hide in, coral reefs themselves become home to hundreds of different plants and animals, *including one-third of all the known 20,000 fish species.* Emperor angelfish, with their slim bodies, for example, elude predators by swiftly darting through the twists and turns; sea horses use their tails to anchor themselves right to the coral and then change color to blend in. Rose coral is a favorite hideout for scallops that tuck themselves in between its "petals."

But the one predator that animals living in a coral reef are hard-pressed to escape from is humans! Some of the world's richest reefs, between the Indonesian and Philippine islands, have been largely destroyed by cyanide poisoning. In the 1960s, fishermen selling live marine animals to the aquarium industry began squirting that chemical on coral colonies. Then they'd pry apart the reef with crowbars to get at the stunned fish hiding behind it! (Can you imagine?) Cyanide fishing, as well as *blast fishing* (also called *fish bombing*) with deadly explosives (a method that has put more than 80 percent of Indonesia's reefs at risk), is now illegal.

A single blast can destroy thousands of years of coral growth. But enforcing the law across the international waters of a huge ocean is very difficult. The good news is that a conservation group called the International Marinelife Alliance is retraining poison fishermen to use hand-carried nets.

A MAGICAL WONDERLAND

If you ever get the chance to go snorkeling with a reputable snorkeling guide near some coral colonies, go for it! What awaits you are all kinds of coral and colorful fish that most of us only see in books or at aquariums. It's a beautiful sight and you can snorkel without disturbing the coral or the fish. What's more, you may want to join an organization such as the **Coral Reef Rehabilitation Project** or even do research on coral farming.

Cool!!!

FOSSIL FUELS

Not all of the ocean's resources come right out of the water — some come from *under* it. Sandwiched between layers of rock under the seafloor near the continents are ancient sea creatures and dinosaurs (no kidding!). And guess what? After being heated and pressurized for millions of years they have turned to petroleum oil and natural gas (you can see why we call them *fossil fuels*). Almost a third of the world's oil is pumped from these offshore reserves, particularly ones that have been discovered in the Arabian Gulf, the North Sea (between Great Britain and Norway), and the Gulf of Mexico. To tap into them, enormous drilling rigs — some as big as cities — are towed to the site and supported by huge stiltlike legs that rest directly on the ocean floor. The production platforms are raised so far above sea level, even rough waves from big ocean storms don't stop production.

Is this a good thing? Oil and natural gas are sure important to our way of life. And what harm could it cause the ocean? Well, you decide.

Ocean Gazette

**March 24, 1989:
Grounded Oil Tanker Pours Crude Oil into Prince William Sound**

The Exxon Valdez tanker hit bottom and became stuck on Bligh Reef today, rupturing eight of its 11 cargo tanks and causing nearly 11 million gallons (40 million L) of crude (unprocessed) oil — that's enough to fill 500 swimming pools! — to spill into Alaska's Prince William Sound in the Gulf of Alaska. Crew members describe the grounding, which occurred at 12:04 A.M., as a bumpy ride consisting of six very sharp jolts. The suspected cause of the accident was human fatigue and error. Captain Joseph Hazelwood had been drinking alcoholic beverages earlier that day and left command of the ship to Third Mate Gregory Cousins who was not certified to handle the ship through the Sound. Cousins had been awake and generally on duty for up to 18 hours prior to the grounding.

Rescuing oiled birds in Prince William Sound, Alaska, after the *Exxon Valdez* spill

SPOILED BY OIL

Because the ocean is as huge as it is, you may think that something that happens in one small part of it like the Gulf of Alaska won't have much of an effect on the rest. But remember those ocean currents! They can carry pollutants thousands of miles (km) around the world. When crude oil spills from a tanker or an offshore oil well, it often catches fire or partially evaporates. In both cases, it releases gases into the atmosphere that contribute to acid rain and global warming. Then, the heavier sticky part of the oil (called *mousse*) sinks to the ocean floor or washes up on coastlines where it can poison or suffocate the wildlife living there — especially shellfish that are just too slow to escape. Animals whose fur or feathers get coated with oil lose their ability to keep warm (or fly), and that can prove fatal in cold climates. As a result of the *Exxon Valdez* spill, some 15,000 otters died of poisoning or hypothermia! You can find out all about what caused the *Exxon Valdez* spill and the cleanup attempt that followed at **<www.oilspill.state.ak.us/facts/details.html>**.

SOME OF THE WORLD'S WORST OIL SPILLS

While the Exxon Valdez *accident is generally considered to have caused more damage to the environment than any other oil spill, dozens more have been far larger*

Vessel	Date	Location	Cause	Gallons (L) of Oil Spilled	Damage
Amoco Cadiz	1978	The waters off the coast of France	Ran aground	68 million gallons (252 million L) of crude oil	Polluted 200 miles (322 km) of sandy beaches and rocky shores, contaminating shellfish beds and oiling an estimated 5,000 seabirds and several tons (t) of fish, as well as marsh grasses and other plants.
Torrey Canyon	1967	Waters near Land's End, England	Ran aground	29 million gallons (107 million L) of crude oil	Polluted the Cornwall and Devon beaches, oiling an estimated 15,000 to 20,000 seabirds.
Sea Empress	1996	Port of Milford Haven, Wales	Ran aground	21 million gallons (78 million L) of crude oil	Polluted 175 miles (282 km) of coastline, destroying fish eggs, fish larvae, and mollusks, and oiling an estimated 20,000 or more seabirds as well as eelgrass beds that may not recover for centuries.

Cleanup an Oil Spill

Even though oil and water don't mix, a spill at sea can be very difficult to cleanup, even with the booms (temporary floating barriers), scrapers, and pumps that environmental cleanup crews use. One of the biggest and most immediate challenges is containing the spill before it spreads over miles (km) of open ocean or is carried ashore where fish, birds, and other coastal wildlife are most likely to be affected.

WHAT YOU NEED

- ⚓ Large baking pan
- ⚓ Water
- ⚓ Scissors
- ⚓ 2 drinking straws
- ⚓ String
- ⚓ 1 teaspoon (5 ml) of vegetable oil
- ⚓ Spoon
- ⚓ Cotton balls
- ⚓ Cornstarch

WHAT YOU DO

1. Fill the pan with about 2" (5 cm) of water. While you wait for it to become still, make a plastic boom by snipping the drinking straws in half and threading the pieces onto a long piece of string.

2. Slowly pour the vegetable oil onto the water surface in the middle of the pan. Now see if you can contain the spill by lowering your boom into the water around the oil and then gently pulling the ends of the string together to close the barrier.

3. Once the oil is contained, you can try to recover it (remove it from the water). For starters, see how much you can skim out with a spoon or soak up with a cotton ball. Finally, sprinkle on some cornstarch. Give it a minute or two to absorb some oil, and carefully scoop out as much as you can. Which method do you think was most effective?

4. Now that you've attempted to clean up an oil spill on a calm day, try it again when the water is choppy. Add more oil and rock the pan a bit to get some wave action going. Good luck!

So, now that you see what oil can do to water, what do you think of drilling in the ocean for fossil fuels?

GLOBAL TEMPS ARE ON THE RISE

You know how hot it gets inside a car that's been parked in the sun for a long time: The windows let the sunlight in, but they also keep the heat from escaping. The glass panels of a greenhouse do the same thing — and because plants love light and warmth, they grow like crazy! And that's a good thing.

Now, certain gases in the earth's atmosphere act like a giant greenhouse by absorbing and trapping heat from the sun. If they didn't, it'd be way too cold for us to live here — so that's a good thing, too! But here's the hitch: We humans do lots of things that increase the levels of these *greenhouse gases*. Whenever we use electricity generated by fossil fuels, heat our houses, drive cars, or do anything else that burns fossil fuels or wood, we're bumping up the levels of carbon dioxide (CO_2) and nitrous oxide (N_2O). Plus, our landfills, farms, and factories emit methane, another greenhouse gas.

At this point, greenhouse gases are doing *too* good of a job! The earth's not just keeping warm, it's heating up at an increasingly fast rate, which scientists call *global warming*. And as temperatures rise, so will the sea level. And you already know why! First, because melting polar ice caps will add great volumes of liquid to the ocean; second, because water itself expands as it warms. Scientists expect at least a 6" to 12" (15 to 30 cm) rise in the ocean level in the next 100 years. That may not sound like a lot, but it's enough to flood miles and miles (km) of shoreline — and seriously impact some 3 billion people who live in coastal regions. And remember how strong water is (page 38)? Well, imagine how those shore homes are going to fare.

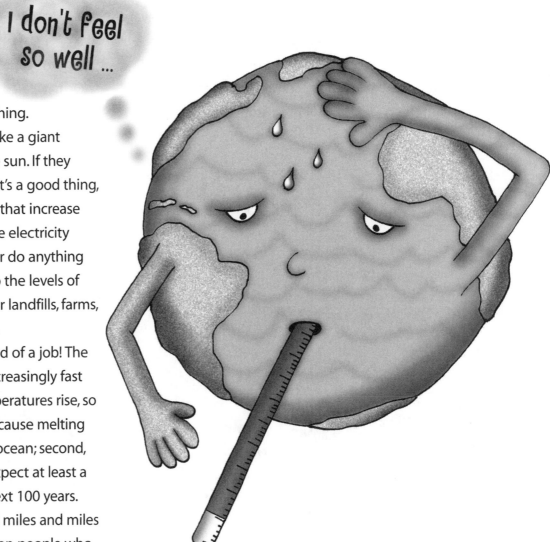

I don't feel so well ...

"I Think I'll Walk"

There are lots of little ways you can make sure you *don't* do your part when it comes to contributing to global warming. Whenever practical, go with the choice that uses less fossil fuel — like walking or biking instead of riding in a car. And get in the habit of turning off lights and electronic equipment, such as your stereo, television, and computer, as soon as you've stopped using them.

Planting a tree can help, too. Trees and other shrubs and plants absorb carbon dioxide from the air.

Try This! For fun, try to see how long you can go from Saturday morning to Monday morning without using fossil fuels. Or, have a contest at home to see who saves the most by scoring a point every time you turn off lights, walk and don't ride, or put on a sweater instead of turning up the heat. How'd you do?

Ocean Gazette

January 24, 2002:
Antarctica Is Warming Up!

According to a scientific report released today, Antarctica's lakes aren't staying frozen as many weeks per year as they used to. The warmer water temperatures seem to suit the resident phytoplankton, whose numbers have steadily increased, but experts from the Intergovernmental Panel on Climate Change are worried. If rising global temperatures eventually cause Antarctica to lose all of its ice, the sea level could rise as much as 213' (65 m). In the last 10 years already, three of that continent's ice shelves have already crumbled and two more are expected to break up soon.

Piles of Plastic

It's no wonder that plastic has become such a popular packing material with manufacturers. It doesn't cost much to make, it's lightweight, and it's *durable* (longlasting) — so durable that it doesn't easily break down, or *degrade*. There lies the dilemma, especially since so much packaging is used only once and then thrown away.

About a fourth of the trash in our landfills is made of plastic. And tons (t) more end up in the ocean every year — discarded or lost overboard, or carried in rivers and streams. Once it's there, many animals mistake it for food; and because they can't digest it, it piles up in their stomachs. The result? The animals end up starving, because their "tummies" tell them they are full — full of plastic, that is.

Nylon netting lost or tossed from fishing boats present a real hazard, too, because it goes right on catching fish! Even larger animals, such as seals and turtles, can get tangled and drown in these "ghost nets."

The plastic yokes that hold together beverage cans are equally dangerous, especially to seals and shore birds that get their heads and legs caught in them. You can help prevent ocean animals from being strangled or drowned by snipping through the rings of any plastic yoke before disposing of it in the trash.

Try This! Most of us don't realize how much *nonbiodegradable* (doesn't break down) plastic we use on a regular basis. For one day, make a list of every little thing you touch that's made from plastic, from the milk jug and margarine container to the television and the phone. Don't forget your toothbrush! How many items on your list get used just once before they're thrown away? Can you think of better packaging alternatives or ways those items could be reused?

THE RECYCLE CYCLE

In the 1990s, people became very involved in recycling, but now some people and places are not recycling because they say it costs too much. And some of these places are big cities! Would you believe that New York City has just stopped recycling glass and plastic beverage bottles? What about where you live? Here's something every person who reads this book can do: Find out if your town or city recycles and, if not, write your mayor, your governor, and your congressperson in protest!

THE INTERNATIONAL COASTAL CLEANUP

Every September, kids from around the world and their families lend a hand in the International Coastal Cleanup sponsored by the The Ocean Conservancy (headquarters in Washington, D.C.) You can find more about this popular event at <www.coastalcleanup.org>.

Raise Awareness

Start an Ocean Log

Every day there's some breaking news about the ocean: stories that range from how thousands of sea jelly fossils were discovered in a Wisconsin quarry where they washed up during a freak ocean storm some 500 million years ago, to how rising sea surface temperatures will cause intense hurricanes over the next few decades. And because scientists believe the ocean is home to many more species yet to be discovered, plenty more news is bound to follow — some fun, some awesome, some sad, and some demanding action!

(If you live near a lake or river, you might want to keep a river or lake log. You can be certain that problems will need attention. Look in your local newspaper for articles to clip.)

To keep track of it all, start a personalized ocean log. All you need is a blank book like a diary. Decorate the cover by gluing on an ocean picture or postcard, or design your own cover. Then, every time you come across an interesting newspaper story, clip it out and paste it in your log. (You can also check the news online — a good source is **<www.seasky.org/sea.html>**.) In this way, you'll

be creating an ongoing time line. With each addition, jot down your own predictions of what may happen next. Or brainstorm ideas for environmental problems that have arisen. Let your voice be heard through letters and e-mails. Who knows? You and your friends may be the ones to come up with a solution.

(111)

Ocean Gazette

July 25, 2002:
Navy Up Against a
Whale of a Dilemma

One thing the U.S. Navy is not keeping quiet about these days is testing out a new method for spying on enemy submarines. These sub-detection techniques, called Low-Frequency Active sonar, flood a huge area of the ocean with intense noise. These tests are so noisy, in fact, that the Natural Resources Defense Council (NRDC) plans to challenge the Navy in U.S. District Court to prevent it from conducting them. The NRDC is concerned that the tests — which are performed in coastal waters with large sea life populations — will drastically affect nearby whales that rely on sound to navigate their way through the ocean, find food and care for their young, and communicate with each other.

Fish for Facts

Suppose you are heading up a committee to gather information to bring the public up to date quickly on the controversy surrounding the possible impact of the Navy's sub-detection testing on whales and other sea life. You've assembled a panel of leading experts — engineers, technicians, Navy officials, and marine biologists.

Here's what you know already:

- During a four- to five-hour period, the Navy dropped 12 *sonobuoys* (the devices designed to detect submarines) in the waters off Great Abaco Island in the Bahamas.

- Within two days of the exercises, 14 whales grounded themselves on beaches 35' to 70' (11 to 21 m) away from where the sonobuoys were dropped.

- Whale beachings in the Bahamas generally occur about once in a decade.

- The Navy reports that it followed all standard environmental precautions, including flying over the area to look for marine mammals prior to testing and comparing the sound levels of the tests with those considered safe for marine mammal species.

Think about what questions you'd want to pose to the panel to better determine if the Navy's testing really is posing a threat to whale populations — and, if so, what possible solutions could be explored.

Make Sea Tees

A fun — and stylish — way to raise public awareness about the ocean is to design a T-shirt that delivers an important message. Consider making a bunch of them to sell and then donating the profits to an environmental organization, like Greenpeace, that works to preserve ocean resources and protect marine animals.

Start by brainstorming slogans that get a message across about the ocean in a fun or clever way. Go with something that's short enough to read quickly. Here are a few ideas to get you started:

KEEP THE OCEAN CLEAN

A SHORE THING: WE NEED THE OCEAN

WE'D FLOUNDER WITHOUT THE SEA

IT'S PLAIN TO SEE WE NEED THE SEA!

Once you've chosen a favorite, think of possible designs that might work well with it and sketch some samples on paper. Perhaps you can incorporate a certain letter into a simple drawing of a sea creature. For example, an *L* might become a fish tail if you tilt it slightly. Or an *O* could be the head of an octopus! Resketch your design onto adhesive-backed paper, then cut out all the pieces.

Next, trim a piece of cardboard to fit inside a clean, dry white T-shirt (this creates a nice flat working surface and will keep color from seeping through to the back of the shirt when you start painting). Peel the backing off the cutouts and stick the shapes securely onto the shirt.

For the ocean, put a few separate blobs of ocean-colored fabric paint on a paper plate. It'll look really cool if you use a few different shades of blue and even a bit of green! Wet a sponge and squeeze it out well. Then press it lightly into the paint and sponge-paint bubbly water onto the shirt right over the cutouts.

Once the paint has dried, peel the cutouts from the shirt. (It's OK if the edges aren't crisp.) Now, use fabric paint or pens to fill in your design. (Be sure to read the paint manufacturer's directions before washing your shirt.)

113

EPILOGUE

Now you know what an important role the ocean plays in all of our lives, even if you don't happen to live anywhere near it, or have never seen it in person. Without the ocean, the earth would lose its cool! By circulating warm water from the equator and cold water from the poles, the ocean keeps our earth from getting sizzling hot — too hot for us to live on. Plus, it affects the weather, supplies us with food and other resources (like salt, fresh water, and fuel), and offers opportunities for good fun and adventure.

Unlike the continents, which have been largely explored and charted, the ocean is still a great frontier — where we're likely to encounter all kinds of interesting new plants and animals. Possibly, we'll even discover resources in the ocean to develop new medicines or to harness enough energy to generate all the electricity we need!

In the ocean, all the elements of nature are in balance. Our role, as its protectors, is doing what it takes to keep the sea that way. That's where you come in, Ambassador of the Ocean. In the coming years, you'll be asked to help make important decisions that will determine the fate of the sea.

Sometimes making the right choices will be as easy as going with the flow; other times the best choices may call for swimming against the tide! But if we all do our part, the shores will be the only limit when it comes to future possibilities in this wavy, watery world we all share.

INDEX

MORE GOOD BOOKS FROM WILLIAMSON PUBLISING

Williamson books are available from your bookseller or directly from Williamson Publishing. Please see last page for ordering information or to visit our website. Thank you.

Also by Cindy Littlefield

Williamson's *Kids Can!*® books ...

Kids Can!® books for ages 6 to 14 are 120 to 176 pages, fully illustrated, trade paper, 11 x 8$^1/_2$, $12.95 US/$19.95 CAN.

Fizz, Bubble & Flash

The Curious Kid's HANDS-ON SCIENCE BOOK

Element Explorations & Atomic Adventures

by Anita Brandolini, Ph.D.

Parents' Choice Recommended
Children's Digest Health Award

The Kids' Guide to FIRST AID

All About Bruises, Burns, Stings, Sprains & Other Ouches

by Karen Buhler Gale, R.N.

Parents' Choice Recommended

THE KIDS' BOOK OF WEATHER FORECASTING

Build a Weather Station, "Read" the Sky & Make Predictions!

with meteorologist Mark Breen and Kathleen Friestad

Parents' Choice Honor Award

THE KIDS' NATURAL HISTORY BOOK

Making Dinos, Fossils, Mammoths & More

by Judy Press

Parents' Choice Honor Award
American Institute of Physics Science Writing Award

GIZMOS & GADGETS

Creating Science Contraptions that Work (& Knowing Why)

by Jill Frankel Hauser

American Bookseller Pick of the Lists
Benjamin Franklin Best Juvenile Nonfiction Award

SUPER SCIENCE CONCOCTIONS

50 Mysterious Mixtures for Fabulous Fun

by Jill Frankel Hauser

American Bookseller Pick of the Lists
Oppenheim Toy Portfolio Best Book

THE KIDS' SCIENCE BOOK

Creative Experiences for Hands-On Fun

by Robert Hirschfeld and Nancy White

Parents' Choice Gold Award
Dr. Toy Best Vacation Product

THE KIDS' NATURE BOOK

365 Indoor/Outdoor Activities & Experiences

by Susan Milord

THE KIDS' WILDLIFE BOOK

Exploring Animal Worlds through Indoor/Outdoor Experiences

by Warner Shedd

American Bookseller Pick of the Lists
Skipping Stones Nature & Ecology Honor Award

EcoArt!

Earth-Friendly Art & Craft Experiences for 3- to 9-Year-Olds

by Laurie Carlson

GREAT GAMES!

Ball, Board, Quiz & Word, Indoors & Out, for Many or Few!

by Sam Taggar

Awesome Ocean Science!

American Bookseller Pick of the Lists
Parents' Choice Approved

SUMMER FUN!

60 Activities for a Kid-Perfect Summer

by Susan Williamson

Selection of Book-of-the-Month; Scholastic Book Clubs

KIDS COOK!

Fabulous Food for the Whole Family

by Sarah Williamson and Zachary Williamson

Parents' Choice Approved

BOREDOM BUSTERS!

The Curious Kids' Activity Book

by Avery Hart and Paul Mantell

Parents' Choice Approved
Dr. Toy Best Vacation Product

KIDS GARDEN!

The Anytime, Anyplace Guide to Sowing & Growing Fun

by Avery Hart and Paul Mantell

Parents Magazine Parents' Pick

KIDS LEARN AMERICA!

Bringing Geography to Life with People, Places & History

by Patricia Gordon and Reed C. Snow

 Williamson's *Kaleidoscope Kids®* **books …**

Kaleidoscope Kids® books for children, ages 7 to 14, are 96–112 pages, two-color, fully illustrated, 10 x 10, $12.95 US/ $19.95 CAN .

Teachers' Choice Award

GEOLOGY ROCKS!

50 Hands-On Activities to Explore the Earth

by Cindy Blobaum

THE LEWIS & CLARK EXPEDITION

Join the Corps of Discovery to Explore Uncharted Territory

by Carol A. Johmann

Benjamin Franklin Silver Award

GOING WEST!

Journey on a Wagon Train to Settle a Frontier Town

by Carol A. Johmann and Elizabeth J. Rieth

Children's Book Council Notable Book

WHO *REALLY* DISCOVERED AMERICA?

Unraveling the Mystery & Solving the Puzzle

by Avery Hart

ANCIENT ROME!

Exploring the Culture, People & Ideas of This Powerful Empire

by Avery Hart and Sandra Gallagher

American Bookseller Pick of the Lists

ANCIENT GREECE!

40 Hands-On Activities to Experience This Wondrous Age

by Avery Hart and Paul Mantell

Children's Book Council Notable Book
Dr. Toy 10 Best Educational Products

PYRAMIDS!

50 Hands-On Activities to Experience Ancient Egypt

by Avery Hart and Paul Mantell

Children's Book Council Notable Book
American Bookseller Pick of the Lists

KNIGHTS & CASTLES

50 Hands-On Activities to Experience the Middle Ages

by Avery Hart and Paul Mantell

American Bookseller Pick of the Lists

¡MEXICO!

40 Activities to Experience Mexico Past & Present

by Susan Milord

ForeWord Magazine Book of the Year Finalist

SKYSCRAPERS!

Super Structures to Design & Build

by Carol A. Johmann

Parents' Choice Recommended

BRIDGES!

Amazing Structures to Design, Build & Test

by Carol A. Johmann and Elizabeth J. Rieth

THE BEAST IN YOU!

Activities & Questions to Explore Evolution

by Marc McCutcheon

Williamson's _Quick Starts for Kids!_® books …

Quick Starts for Kids!® books for children, ages 8 to 80, are each 64 pages, fully illustrated, trade paper, 8 x 10, $7.95 US/$10.95 CAN.

Dr. Toy 100 Best Children's Products
Dr. Toy 10 Best Socially Responsible Products
MAKE YOUR OWN BIRDHOUSES & FEEDERS
by Robyn Haus

GARDEN FUN!
Indoors & Out; In Pots & Small Spots
by Vicky Congdon

KIDS' EASY BIKE REPAIRS
Tune-Ups, Tools & Quick Fixes
by Stephen Cole

MAKE MAGIC!
50 Tricks to Mystify & Amaze
by Ron Burgess

DRAWING HORSES
(that look real!)
by Don Mayne

Visit Our Website!

To see what's new at Williamson and learn more about specific books, visit our website at: **www.williamsonbooks.com**

Oppenheim Toy Portfolio Gold Award
DRAW YOUR OWN CARTOONS!
by Don Mayne

40 KNOTS TO KNOW
Hitches, Loops, Bends & Bindings
by Emily Stetson

MAKE YOUR OWN FUN PICTURE FRAMES!
by Matt Phillips

MAKE YOUR OWN HAIRWEAR
Beaded Barrettes, Clips, Dangles & Headbands
by Diane Baker

Parents' Choice Approved
BAKE THE BEST-EVER COOKIES!
by Sarah A. Williamson

BE A CLOWN!
Techniques from a Real Clown
by Ron Burgess

YO-YO!
Tips & Tricks from a Pro
by Ron Burgess

KIDS' EASY KNITTING PROJECTS
by Peg Blanchette

Be a Williamson You Can Do It!™ Winner!

SEND IN YOUR PROJECT PHOTOS AND WRITINGS TO ENTER!
NOW you can see selected projects from readers just like you posted on our website! And one project per month will be named a _You Can Do It!™_ winner. The winning child, family, or group will receive a gift certificate for Williamson books (that the winner can select)!

Visit our website to see how to enter the Williamson _You Can Do It!™_ contest. Once you enter, visit our website to see if your project is posted and to see if you are a Williamson Winner: www.williamsonbooks.com.

Free Teacher's Guides!

If you are a schoolteacher or are homeschooling your family, please visit our website <www.williamsonbooks.com> and click on "For Teachers, Parents & Caregivers" to download FREE Teacher's Guides with additional classroom ideas, activities, and projects.

To Order Books:

You'll find Williamson books wherever high-quality children's books are sold, or order directly from Williamson Publishing.
   We accept Visa and MasterCard _(please include the number and expiration date and your phone number)._

Order on our secure website:
www.williamsonbooks.com

Toll-free phone orders with credit cards: **1-800-234-8791**

Toll-free fax orders: **1-800-304-7224**

Or, send a check with your order to:
Williamson Publishing Company
P.O. Box 185
Charlotte, Vermont 05445

Catalog request: **web, mail, phone, or e-mail <info@williamsonbooks.com>**

Please add **$4.00** for postage for one book plus **$1.00** for each additional book. Satisfaction is guaranteed or full refund on books without questions or quibbles.